Iceland

by Ann F Stonehouse

Ann Stonehouse is an experienced writer and editor with a wide range of interests, from travel and literature to Scottish fiddle music. She has contributed to many books, including the AA's *Great Voyages of the World*, and her photos have appeared in a recent guide to Antarctica.

Above: the peak of *Vindbelgjar looms above the northeastern shore of Mývatn*

AA Publishing

Written by Ann F Stonehouse

First published 2001
Reprinted Feb 2002; April 2003
Reprinted 2004. Information verified and updated.
Reprinted Dec 2004
Reprinted May and Aug 2005

Iceland's team of huskies
taking a well-earned rest

© Automobile Association Developments Limited 2004
Maps © Automobile Association Developments Limited 2003

Published by AA Publishing, a trading name of Automobile Association Developments Limited, whose registered office is Southwood East, Apollo Rise, Farnborough, Hampshire GU14 0JW.
Registered number 1878835.

A CIP catalogue record for this book is available from the British Library.

A02738

Colour separation: Chroma Graphics (Overseas) Pte Ltd, Singapore

Printed and bound in Italy by Printer Trento Srl

Find out more about AA Publishing and the wide range of travel publications and services the AA provides by visiting our website at www.theAA.com/bookshop

Contents

About this Book

KEY TO SYMBOLS

✚ map reference to the maps found in the What to See section

✉ address or location

☎ telephone number

⏰ opening times

🍴 restaurant or café on premises or near by

🚇 nearest underground train station

🚌 nearest bus/tram route

🚉 nearest overground train station

🛳 ferry crossings and boat excursions

ℹ tourist information

♿ facilities for visitors with disabilities

✋ admission charge

⟷ other places of interest near by

❓ other practical information

➤ indicates the page where you will find a fuller description

✈ travel by air

This book is divided into five sections to cover the most important aspects of your visit to Iceland.

Viewing Iceland pages 5–10
An introduction to Iceland by the author.
　The 10 Essentials
　The Shaping of Iceland
　Iceland's Famous

Top Ten pages 11–22
The author's choice of the Top Ten places to see in Iceland, listed in alphabetical order, each with practical information.

What to See pages 23–72
The three main areas of Iceland, each with its own brief introduction and an alphabetical listing of the main attractions.
　Practical information
　Snippets of 'Did you know…' information
　2 suggested drives
　2 suggested walks
　2 features

Where To… pages 73–86
Detailed listings of the best places to eat, stay, shop, take the children and be entertained.

Practical Matters pages 87–92
A highly visual section containing essential travel information.

Maps
All map references are to the individual maps found in the What to See section of this guide.
For example, Hekla has the reference
✚ 24C2 – indicating the page on which the map is located and the grid square in which the volcano is to be found. A list of the maps that have been used in this travel guide can be found in the index.

Prices
Where appropriate, an indication of the cost of an establishment is given by **£** signs:
£££ denotes higher prices, **££** denotes average prices, while **£** denotes lower charges.

Star Ratings
Most of the places described in this book have been given a separate rating:
✪✪✪　　Do not miss
✪✪　　Highly recommended
✪　　Worth seeing

Viewing
Iceland

Above: *Jón Gunnar
Árnarson's sculpture Sólfar,
on the shore at Reykjavík*
Right: *a friendly
welcome for
strangers*

Ann Stonehouse's Iceland

Icelanders

Some 285,000 people live here (60 per cent in the greater Reykjavík area), so it's hardly crowded and there's a relaxed attitude to life, with little crime. Icelandic is related to Old Norse, and English is widely spoken as a second language. People live in little towns and settlements around the fertile perimeter – nobody lives in the rocky desert of the interior, which is accessible only in high summer.

Icelandic Alphabet

Icelandic has two unusual letters. In this book we have used Ð/ð (more properly ð), which is pronounced as a hard 'th'; but we have replaced Þ/þ, which can be confused with the Roman letter 'P', with 'th' (► also 92).

Standing on the edge of Vatnajökull, the largest glacier in Europe

First-time visitors arriving at Keflavík airport look out on the surprisingly fresh-looking lunar landscape of Iceland and wonder what they've done. Most, like me, find themselves hooked and come back again and again.

At a mere 20 million years old, it's the youngest country in Europe, an island just bigger than Ireland (350km from south to north, 540km from west to east) and lying across the vast undersea split known as the Mid-Atlantic Ridge, where two of the great plates of the earth's surface are pulling apart. This makes it one of the most volcanically active sites, a geography lesson brought to life, but it is a land with so much more to offer than that. It's a great place for outdoor activities – hiking, horse riding, fishing and winter sports to name a few. It's an important breeding place for many rare birds, blessed with sparkling clean air, the 'midnight sun' and endless summer days (come in mid-winter for the Northern Lights). The mountains, fjords, rivers and waterfalls provide sweeping landscapes and an unexpectedly diverse flora.

The living is expensive when so much is imported, and tourist facilities are usually sound rather than luxurious. The changeable weather and unmade roads are notorious but they won't stop you getting to most places, summer or winter. Don't try to see everything in one visit – the ring road looks a temptingly short way to get around, but if you don't stop and explore properly you'll have missed most of what Iceland really has to offer. And the rewards are fantastic.

THE **10** ESSENTIALS

Everything about Iceland is fascinating but there are certain experiences which should not be missed. Below are some of the essentials:

• **Eat fish** – there's a great selection of top restaurants to choose from. Try Við Tjörnina in Reykjavík (➤ 76), or Viðeyjarstofan on Viðey (➤ 76) for the best.
• **Get off the Hringvegur (ring road)** into the mountains and the interior – and if the bumpy state of the side roads puts you off, enjoy the advantages of an organised tour.
• **Take the lift** to the top of the Hallgrímskirkja tower for the best views over Reykjavík (➤ 16).
• **Go for a ride** on an Icelandic horse and try the unique 'fifth gait' for yourself – it's a leisurely way to explore the countryside.

• **Explore a steaming geothermal area** to understand why Iceland is as it is.
• **Talk to the locals** for real insights – Icelanders have a keen national identity and pride, and are usually pleased to tell you more about their country.
• **Watch puffins**, everybody's favourite sea bird.
• **Relax in a thermally heated 'hot-pot'**; they don't come more comfortable than the Blue Lagoon (➤ 12) but local swimming pools have them too.

Discovering the countryside on horseback

• **Treat yourself to a trip onto a glacier** by snow-scooter or snow-tractor. Vatnajökull is the biggest in Europe but there are plenty of other choices.
• **Visit a Reykjavík sculpture gallery** and get to know more about Icelandic art – there's public sculpture everywhere and it's more fun if you know what you're looking at.

Left: riding a snow scooter on Vatnajökull
Below: a hissing steam vent at Námafjall, near Lake Mývatn

The Shaping of Iceland

4th century BC
Greek explorer Pytheas describes a country six days' sailing north from Britain, which he calls Thule.

6th century BC
Irish abbot St Brendan sails north to discover a mysterious 'paradise of birds' and 'flaming mountains', believed to be an early sighting of Iceland.

c AD 700
Irish monks settle along the southern coastline.

800–1066
Norwegian expansionist policies result in the violent Viking Age of exploration and settlement, marked by exodus from Britain, Ireland and Scandinavia.

874
Norwegian Ingólfur Arnarson becomes the First Settler, choosing Reykjavík. Followed by farmers from Norway and Britain.

930
Parliamentary system of government introduced with a national assembly, the Althing. Thorsteinn Ingólfsson rules with 48 chiefs and 96 advisers.

1000
Althing agrees, under Norwegian pressure, to adopt Christianity. Judiciously, pagan worship is still permitted at home. Bishoprics established at Skálholt and Hólar.

1200–20
Writing of the Sagas (heroic narratives) telling of the great families who lived in Iceland from 930–1030.

1262
Riven by internal fighting and desperate for peace, Iceland

A romanticised view of Iceland's first settlers

negotiates Norwegian rule. Effects of excessive taxes in a time of hardship are exacerbated by widespread disease.

14th century
Devastation of the southwest follows several eruptions of Hekla. With the union of Scandinavian countries at Kalmar, Iceland passes to Danish rule.

1550
Catholic bishop Jón Arason, the last bastion against Lutheranism, is beheaded at Skálholt.

end 16th century
Consecutive harsh winters cause widespread famine, and over 9,000 Icelanders die.

1602
Foreign trade is monopolised by the Danish crown, holding back economic development.

1703
First census shows Iceland's population to be just over 50,000, mostly farming.

1783
Erruption of Laki (Lakakígar) over ten months devastates the southeast. In the famine which follows, 20 per cent of the population die.

1855
Efforts of scholar Jón Sigurðsson bring about restoration of free trade.

1870
Start of large-scale migration to North America.

1874
Althing gains domestic rule from Denmark.

1901
British and Danish governments set a fishing limit of 6km around Iceland.

National feeling ran high during the 'Cod Wars'

1973
Major erruption on Heimaey, with much of a town buried under lava. A tax of 2 per cent on all Icelanders helps the subsequent rebuilding.

1980
Vigdís Finnbogadóttir becomes the first female elected head of state in the world.

1989
The sale of beer is legalised.

1911
University of Iceland is founded in Reykjavík.

1940
German occupation of Denmark in April ends union with Iceland. In May, British troops occupy the island as a strategic air base.

1941
US takes over defence, moving in some 60,000 troops. This brings prosperity, employment and high inflation.

1944
On 17 June the Republic of Iceland is formally established at Thingvellir.

1949
Iceland joins NATO, with agreement that foreign troops will not be stationed there in peacetime. However, in 1951 the US establishes an apparently permanent base at Keflavík.

1963–65
Erruption on the seabed and appearance of a new island, Surtsey.

1972–76
'Cod Wars' with UK as Iceland declares a fishing limit of 80km, and then 320km. Britain concedes after clashes between Icelandic gun-boats and British warships.

1992
In disagreement over commercial whaling rights, Iceland leaves the International Whaling Convention and joins the rival North Atlantic Marine Mammal Commission, with Norway and the Faroes, but does not resume whaling.

1996
Grímsvötn erupts beneath Vatnajökull, releasing floods which sweep away roads and bridges.

2000
Reykjavík selected as European City of Culture 2000.

Iceland's Famous

Leifur Eiríksson (fl. AD 1000)

Eldest son of banished Icelandic Viking Erik the Red, 'Leif the Lucky' is widely credited with the earliest European discovery of North America. He set sail from Greenland around AD 1000 with 35 followers, and is believed to have made landings on Baffin Island ('Helluland') and down the east coast to the tip of Newfoundland ('Vínland') before returning safely with claims of a lush land of paradise.

Snorri Sturluson (1179–1241)

Snorri was a wealthy and powerful chief, Lawspeaker at the Althing and a descendant of the Viking hero and skaldic poet Egill Skallagrímson. He wrote the great Icelandic *Prose Edda* (a recording of Norse mythology), *Heimskringla* (the history of Norwegian kings) and probably *Egil's Saga* as well. He farmed around Borgarfjörður and Reykholt, and was murdered by Norwegian agents in 1241.

Halldór Laxness (1902–98)

Born in Reykjavík, Halldór Laxness travelled widely as a young man to Scandinavia, Germany and the USA. His first novel, *Child of Nature*, was published when he was just 17. He went on to write many stories, essays and poems, and was awarded the Nobel Prize for Literature in 1955. His best-known novel is *Independent People* (1946), set in the early 20th century, which gives a realistically grim insight into peasant farming in Iceland up to that period through the tale of the stubborn survivor, Bjartur of Summerhouses.

The statue of Snorri Sturluson at Reykholt

Keiko
Iceland's most famous international film star Keiko the killer whale was first captured off Iceland in 1979 and later plucked from obscurity in a US ocean park to star in the film *Free Willy*. An ambitious programme to rehabilitate him into the wild began by returning him to home waters. Nursed back to health in Heimaey Bay, he was finally released in July 2002, and three months later he turned up at Korsnesfjord in western Norway, which has become his adopted home.

Björk has spawned many imitators, known as 'Björkettes'.

Björk Gudmundsdóttir (1966–)

Björk cut her first disc at the age of 11 and became a founder member of the punk-funk band the Sugarcubes, hitting world stardom with their song *Birthday* in 1988. She's since become Iceland's most popular export in her own recording right, with an inimitable vocal style and a constant ability to shock. In 2000 she was awarded a Palme d'Or for her role in the film *Dancer in the Dark*.

Top Ten

Above: *serene icebergs trapped on the lagoon of Jökulsárlón*

Right: *the tower of the Hallgrímskirkja dominates Reykjavík*

1
Bláa Lónið (Blue Lagoon)

Top facilities at Iceland's naturally hot spa

A pool beside a power station in the middle of a windswept lava field sounds missable, but the famous Blue Lagoon is an absolute must.

✚ 24B1

✉ 5km from Grindavík, off Route 43, 45 minutes southwest of Reykjavík

☎ 420 8800; www.bluelagoon.is

🌐 All year, daily

🍴 Snack bar offers sandwiches, coffee and sweets (£). Good restaurant caters for up to 350 (£–££)

🚌 Regular service from main bus station in Reykjavík, also calls in at bigger hotels on request

ℹ Tourist Information, Hafnargötu 6, Grindavík
☎ 420 1109

♿ Few

✋ Moderate

❓ You can hire swimsuits, bath robes and towels. Take shampoo

In fact it's so good, you may want to go several times during your stay, as it's a great way to relax and unwind from all that sightseeing. The pool is actually geothermally-heated seawater, rich in natural minerals, so you feel wonderfully bouyant as you float around in the silky warmth. It's the natural by-product of the nearby Svartsengi power station, usually tactfully hidden in clouds of steam, which uses water straight from 2000m below the ground which is at a much higher temperature. Once it has cooled down, the water is the comfortable temperature of a hot bath and you can simply lie back in the open air and think of Iceland – even if it's snowing on your head! The opacity comes from the natural white silica mud mixed with minerals and an algae, which gives it the trademark milky blue colour, whatever the weather. Buckets of soapy white gunge are placed around the shore – it's a pleasant sludge of the silica and minerals and you can smear it over yourself for glorious exfoliation. It's supposed to be good for skin conditions (there's a special pool dedicated to psoriasis sufferers, who find great relief) and you'll certainly come away with silky-feeling skin.

The bottom is comfortable sand and the water gets no deeper than adult shoulder-height, so non-swimmers can feel confident. However children under the age of 11 must be supervised. There's always a lifeguard on duty, just in case, fully clothed against the elements for it's much colder in the air than in the water. And don't worry about the potentially exposed bit between the communal changing rooms and the pool – you can get into the water inside the building and swim straight out in total comfort.

2
Flatey

This beautiful island in Breiðafjörður bay is one of the prettiest spots in Iceland and an unexpected secret makes it well worth the effort to get there.

Its name tells you there are no exciting natural features in store – Flatey simply means 'flat island' and as you walk up from the harbour there is nothing especially remarkable about the old wooden houses grouped there, gracious and appealing though they are. Take the well-trodden path that leads through the grassy meadowland, bursting with buttercups and patrolled by anxious Arctic terns, which nest on the ground here in large numbers. Look carefully and you may spot the downy grey chicks, but mind your head – the terns can peck you hard and sharp if they think you're getting too close.

This way leads to the wooden church, deceptively modest in its simple lines for the interior is like no other. Most Lutheran churches are free of embellishment but this one has been painted with a rich set of frescoes, depicting local folk in biblical settings. The effect is breathtaking. The brushstrokes are bold and black, the figures vivid and engaging – note a young, unmistakably Icelandic 'Christ the Fisherman' over the altar. The murals are the work of a Spanish–Icelandic painter, Baltasar, who came here in the 1960s and worked for his keep over a period of several years.

The church is not the only surprise on this extraordinary island. Tucked just behind it is a tiny wooden shed – peer through the murky windows and you'll recognise the smallest and oldest library in Iceland, a legacy of Flatey's historic importance as a trading and religious centre. One of the great medieval manuscripts, *Flateyjarbók*, was held here until its dispersal to Denmark – it's now in the Culture House in Reykjavík.

✚ 24B3

✉ Middle of Breiðafjörður bay

🍴 Small restaurant Veitingastofan Vogur (£–££), with limited accommodation, open summer only ☎ 438 1413

🚢 Ferry *Baldur* from Stykkishólmur calls in daily, check sailings locally

ℹ Tourist Information, Borgarbraut, Stykkishólmur ☎ 438 1150/1750

♿ None

↔ Stykkishólmur (► 47)

❓ Look out for white-tailed sea-eagles around the islands of Breiðafjörður

The old houses return to life in the brief summer months

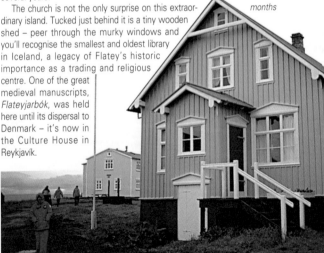

3
Gullfoss & Geysir

✚ 24C2

✉ 125km east of Reykjavík, on Route 35

🕐 Open access

🍴 Hotel and coffee shop with buns at Geysir

🚌 Both sites are included on the classic Golden Circle coach tours, half day or whole day

ℹ Tourist Information Centre, Aðalstræti 2, Reykjavík ☎ 562 3045

♿ Few

✋ Free

A winding path leads down to Gullfoss

Two of Iceland's most spectacular and famous natural sights are found within a few kilometres of each other near the head of a great valley.

Gullfoss is the 'golden waterfall' on the river Hvítá, the most outstandingly beautiful in this land of tumbling water. You can usually see the cloud of vapour and hear the roar long before you see it, set sideways on at the top of a long, narrow gorge which reaches depths of 70m. It is in fact two falls, one immediately above the other and at right angles to it, so you get double the effect. You can view the falls from the railed-off point above or take the path that leads right down to the water, but be warned – you're liable to get wet just from the spray there!

It's hard to imagine anybody wanting to destroy this wonder of nature, but in 1907 it came under threat from developers who sought to contain it for hydroelectric power. They were opposed by a young woman, Sigríður Tómasdóttir, from the neighbouring farm of Brattholt, and her campaign to save the waterfall and its gorge was ultimately successful. She's known as the heroine of the falls and her statue stands by the visitor centre.

In contrast, the spouting steam vents on the hillside at Geysir (pronounced 'gayzeer') have been valued since their first appearance in the 13th century, but alas, the original great Geysir, which gave its name to the phenomenon, no longer blows. It was probably blocked over the centuries by eager sightseers, who threw any handy debris into the bubbling pool to accelerate the spouting. More recent

Strokkur shoots a jet of water high into the air

moves to replumb it have damaged it beyond repair. However, Geysir's smaller neighbour Strokkur is well worth seeing in its own right, and goes off every ten minutes or so, shooting boiling steam some 30m into the air (make sure you stand up-wind). It's fascinating to watch as the water in the circular pool at its base is sucked in and out by the pressure of hot geothermal water and cold river water down below, as though you were standing on the back of a living, breathing monster rather than stone. When the pool is almost full, the water at the centre suddenly bubbles up in a luminous blue swell and the plume of steam erupts with a great hiss – not to be missed.

Blue water wells up just before the geyser erupts

4
Hallgrímskirkja, Reykjavík

✝ 29C1

✉ Skólavörðuholt

☎ 510 1000

🕐 Church May–Sep, daily 9–6; Oct–Apr, daily 9–5; tower daily 10–5

🚌 7

ℹ Tourist Information Centre, Aðalstræti 2
☎ 562 3045

♿ Good

✋ Tower cheap

↔ Safn Einars Jónssonar (Einar Jónsson Sculpture Museum) opposite (➤ 35)

❓ Service Sun 11AM. Regular organ recitals Jul and Aug, Thu and Sat 12:30–1; Sun 8PM

The majestic, sweeping front of the Hallgrímskirkja

Like a giant space shuttle about to take off, the dramatic white tower of the Hallgrímskirkja looms over the old town district of Reykjavík.

Completed in 1974, the church took some 30 years to build, and locals are still getting used to it, but – love it or hate it – you won't get far away from it, for it seems to watch you down every street. It's the most striking modern building in Iceland, was designed by Guðjón Samúelsson (1887–1950), and is named after the 17th-century hymn-writer and poet, the Reverend Hallgrímur Pétursson. It actually stands at the top of Skólavörðustígur and, by the time you have panted your way up the hill, you'll find this a breathtaking building in more senses than one.

While rockets come to mind when you see the church from a distance, close-up its concrete pillars resemble giant hexagonal volcanic columns, or even a fantastical set of organ pipes. Step through the door and it is like being inside a towering ice-cathedral, very cool and unadorned, grey and white, with narrow gothic windows of clear glass showing strips of sky. Turn around and you'll see the huge organ, vulgar by comparison – it boasts 5,275 steely pipes, each sponsored by members of the congregation. The simple furnishings you might expect of a Lutheran church here become minimalist and very stylish. They include a font of clear rock crystal, made in the Czech Republic, and mounted on a block of Icelandic rock. You can take the lift to the 8th floor of the tower, 73m high, for a panorama over the rooftops of Reykjavík. The heroic statue in front of the Hallgrímskirkja is of Leifur Eiríksson (➤ 10).

5
Jökulsárgljúfur

The narrow strip of Jökulsárgljúfur encompasses a magnificent valley, a deep gorge, mysterious echoing rocks and Europe's most powerful waterfall.

The park follows the canyon formed by the Jökulsá á Fjöllum, one of the major rivers which churns northwards from Vatnajökull (► 72). It is believed the canyon was originally formed in the course of a few days, following an explosion of the volcano and subsequent sudden release of meltwater (*jökulhlaup*).

At the park's southern end is Dettifoss, a massive waterfall 45m high and 100m wide, over which the river pours at an incredible rate. It's glacial meltwater, so it's filthy – this is not a pretty waterfall but its power is awesome. You can hear the roar some distance away and when you stand next to it the effect is shattering to the senses (be careful, there are no barriers). There's a footpath down the western side, back to Ásbyrgi, which takes two days to complete, and as you work your way downstream you'll see smaller falls at Hafragilsfoss and Selfoss. If you're not hiking there are plenty of shorter walks to enjoy – leaflets and guides are available from the ranger stations at Ásbyrgi and Vesturdalur.

The half-way point of the canyon is Hólmatungur, lush and green and full of wild flowers in summer. Further north, the strange craggy rocks of Hljóðaklettar, near the Vesturdalur campsite, are famous for their echoes. The northern end of the park at Ásbyrgi is also its most accessible point. Here the canyon opens into a beautiful wide horseshoe shaped valley, reputedly a hoofprint left behind by the god Odin's horse Sleipnir. The high walls protect a basin full of birch and rowan trees, with an outcrop, Eyjan, floating in the middle, a perfect island in a sea of green.

Dettifoss is the highlight of Jökulsárgljúfur, one of only three national parks in Iceland

✚ 25E4

✉ Main entrance from Kelduhverfið, west of Ásbyrgi

☎ 465 2195 (Ásbyrgi campsite)

⊘ Access is limited by the state of the roads, open only in summer

🍴 Café at Ásbyrgi petrol station

ℹ Tourist Information, Hafnarstræti 82, Akureyri ☎ 462 7733; www.eyjafjordur.is

✋ Free

❓ Access roads to west (F862) and east (864). Keep to west for Hljóðaklettar, but road deteriorates to jeep track south of Dettifoss

6
Jökulsárlón

 25E2

Just off Route 1, 75km west of Höfn

Open access

 Small visitor centre and café on site, open in summer

Amphibious vehicle trips leave at regular intervals for a tour of the lake, book at the centre

 Tourist Information Centre, Hafnarbraut 52, Höfn ☎ 478 1500; www.east.is

None

Free

 Often combined on a day tour with a trip up Vatnajökull (➤ 72), expensive but worth it

The icebergs shift gently in the wind and are constantly changing

Icebergs of extraordinary age and beauty float on this glacial lagoon, separated from the sea only by a narrow slip of gravel land.

After the monotony of the surrounding landscape and the coal-black of the *sandur* (glacial gravel) shore, the luminous beauty of the icebergs at Jökulsárlón always surprises. Even on a grey day the compressed ancient turquoise ice, humbug-striped with black glacial morraine, seems to be lit from within as the bergs move in a stately slow dance in the wind. The little that shows on the surface can seem as big as a house, and the view shifts subtly from hour to hour. They are calves of the great Breiðamerjkur glacier which looms up behind, its snout stained black with lava grit. It has been flowing down these mountains for centuries and, as photos in the little café show, it has grown and retreated over the years, gouging a lake 100m deep with icy waters that pour through into the sea. It is in danger of breaking through all together one day, sweeping Route 1 and the fragile suspension bridge with it.

There are good points for photography on both sides of the bridge, and it's worth taking the amphibeous vehicle tour down into the lake to get close amongst the icebergs. You can often see seals fishing in the swift channel, eider ducks swim fearlessly between the shifting ice blocks, and in summer the air is electric with the sharp cries and territorial posturing of Arctic terns. If the tour buses spoil your view, then Breiðarlón is another iceberg lagoon to the south, easily accessed on foot from the main road.

7
Mývatn

Birds in their thousands come to nest in this harmonious conservation area of water and greenery set in an active geothermal area.

It is said that more duck species breed here than anywhere else in the world, 15 in total, including the colourful harlequin, Barrow's goldeneye, scaup, tufted and long-tailed ducks. You'll also find whooper swans, Slavonian grebes and both red-throated and great northern divers. Their breeding ground is mostly to the west of the lake and this area is closed to traffic in high summer.

The birds are part of an ecosystem based on the millions of midges and flies which give the lake its name (pronounced 'meevatn') and also provide food for salmon and char. Their microscopic skeletons have gathered on the lake bottom and support a different economy – diatomite processing in a factory east of Reykjahlið, for use in industrial filters, fertiliser and paint.

The lake averages a depth of only 2.5m and covers some 37sq km. It's in a shallow depression and is full of small green islands. These include many 'pseudo-craters' – looking like mini-volcanoes, they are actually the result of gas-explosions under the lava. Extensive areas show where the rock crust has been cracked by upheavals below, and lava has bubbled up and petrified under the water; Dimmuborgir offers the most spectacular examples of the resulting bizarre natural sculpture.

Námafjall is an extraordinary sulphurous hillside to the east, streaked with red and yellow, with grey boiling mud pools and steam-vents an overwhelming vision of Hell. Exploratory activity at the nearby geothermal power station, Krafla, is believed to have set off more earthquakes.

25D3

99km east of Akureyri

Open access

Several cafés and restaurants around Reykjahlið (£–£££)

Tourist Information Centre in Strax supermarket ☎ 464 4390

None

See drive (➤ 60)

The midges don't bite but do get in your nose, ears, mouth and hair, so a netted hat is recommended for Jun and Aug. Hire a bicycle for leisurely exploration ☎ 464 4220

Camping on the shore of Mývatn

19

8
Skaftafell

Approaching Skaftafell National Park from the west, a panorama of green hills, tumbling ice and gothic mountain pinnacles fills your view.

🕂 25D2

✉ 327km east of Reykjavík

🌐 Open access

ℹ Visitor Centre
   🕐 Summer only
   ☎ 478 1627 🍴 Café
   at visitor centre (£)

♿ None

👋 Free

❓ Mountain guide service
   ☎ 478 1627/894 2959

Stark basalt columns make a dramatic backdrop for the waterfall of Svartifoss in the national park

As you get closer, the scene resolves into three deeply crevassed glaciers, with Skaftafellsjökull flanked by Morsárjökull to the left and Svínafellsjökull to the right, and a fourth, Skeiðarárjökull, much broader and flatter in appearance, over to your left. They are tributaries of the great ice-caps of Vatnajökull and Öræfajökull. You can follow the path up to the snout of Skaftafellsjökull, which pours down into a scenic lake surrounded by surprisingly lush vegetation, but be careful near the glacier where slippery clay overlays the ice under foot. If you want to walk on the glacier itself, make use of the expert ranger service which offers properly guided excursions, hikes and rock climbing.

Sheltered by the mountains, this site gets more than its fair share of good weather but can also catch the rain. The campsite is a very popular place at weekends and so you may prefer to dodge the crowds and come mid-week. In summer the rounded hill behind the visitor centre, Skorar, is covered in birch woods and heath, and there are beautiful walks to the dramatic waterfall of Svartifoss (see walk ► 71) and into the next valley and the mountains behind. The woods are full of twittering redwings. Keep an eye open too for Iceland's smallest bird, a wren (*troglodytes islandicus*), slightly larger than its mainland European cousin.

The braided gravel plain below Skaftafell was the scene of a massive *jökulhlaup* in 1996, when the volcano Grímsvötn erupted beneath Vatnajökull and the resulting flood waters swept away roads and bridges. Trucks and diggers, toy-sized in this vast landscape, constantly shift the gravel around in attempts to limit future damage.

9
Thingvellir

Iceland formed the first parliamentary democracy in the world at Thingvellir, setting a system of government that would last for centuries.

The great fault line at Thingvellir, where the geological plates of America and Europe are tearing slowly apart, provided a remarkable natural arena for the gatherings of freemen, chieftans and bishops to discuss matters of law and justice, crime and punishment. The first Althing, or parliament, was held here in AD 930 and they continued annually (with some breaks) until 1789, when the plain fell 1m in an earthquake and the power base shifted to Reykjavík. The Lawspeaker recited from memory one third of the country's laws each time. You can stand at his rock, marked with a flagpole and wooden platform, and survey the plain below where men would have gathered in temporary turf booths for two weeks each summer, for the social event of the year. Sound echoes off the long line of sheer cliffs behind, making for excellent accoustics.

Birch and willow grow amid the fissured rocks of the plain, with the lake to the south and low mountains in the distance, and the eye is drawn to the 19th-century church and the white-gabled farmhouse beside it. The classic view of the site is from the hill above and to the west, just off Route 36. By the approach to the church, one of the fissures of cold, clear water has become an oracle, with coins gleaming like fishscales at the bottom – ask your question as your coin falls and, if you can see it land on the bottom, the answer is 'yes'.

24B2

49km northeast of Reykjavík on Route 361

Open access

Café (£) at visitor centre

Summer boat trips and fishing on the lake, book at visitor centre

Thjónustumiðstöð (visitor centre for National Park) at junction of routes 36 and 361 ☎ 482 2660/3606; www.thingvellir.is

Free

Included in 'Golden Circle' tours with Gullfoss and Geysir

Good walk along chasm from Hótel Valhöll, past Lawspeaker's rock and the drowning pool Drekkingarhylor to Öxarárfoss waterfall

Thingvellir is a sacred site, and still the venue for major national events

10
Vestmannaeyjar
(Westmann Islands)

✠ 24C1

✉ 11km off south coast

🍴 Full range of eating places on Heimaey (£–£££)

🚢 Ferry from Thorlákshöfn takes 3 hours
☎ 481 2800

✈ Flights from Reykjavik to Heimaey; also sight-seeing flights over Surtsey

ℹ Tourist Information Centre, Básaskersbryggja (ferry terminal), Heimaey
☎ 481 3555/2694

❓ On August nights, look out for children with buckets. They are rescuing fledgling puffin chicks confused by the lights in the town

This intriguing archipelago off the southwest coast includes Surtsey, a new island, and Heimaey, which suffered a devastating eruption in 1973.

The low black wedge of Surtsey emerged from the sea in a spew of flames and ash during the period 1963–6, the result of a submarine volcano on the same great faultline which is splitting the mainland. You can't land – the site is protected so that scientists may study the growth and colonisation of an island which reflects the creation of Iceland itself. Already small plants have taken root and even the first earthworm has been found.

Despite their settled appearance, none of the Westmann Islands is older than 5–10,000 years (infantile in geological terms) and parts of the biggest and only inhabited island, Heimaey (pronounced haymay), are a lot newer than that. The eruption of the volcano here on 23 January 1973 took everybody by surprise, and could be observed from the hills south of Reykjavík. By great luck, the fishing fleet was in and so the population of 5000 was evacuated safely that same night. Then began an epic battle to prevent the town being totally destroyed by lava, which continued to flow for five months; seawater was pumped over it and you can see clearly how it stopped just short of the harbour. In fact, the new rock narrowed the harbour mouth to make it one of the safest anchorages in Iceland.

The gritty lava on Eldfell is still warm to the touch, and hot enough below the surface to bake bread – you can climb it for a great view over the town and of the green amphitheatre of Herjólfsdalur, where locals have their own three-day mega-party, with booze and bonfires, in early August. Look out for puffin hunters on the cliffs opposite the harbour. They are selective in what they catch and make little dent on the population.

Kittiwakes nesting on the cliffs at the harbour entrance, Heimaey

What to See

Above: *garden in the lava*
Right: *a sculpture outside the National Gallery in Reykjavik*

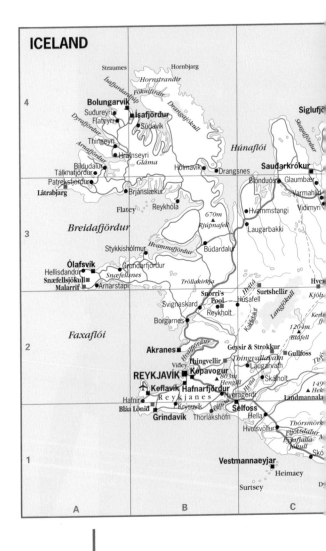

ICELAND

Straumes
Hornbjarg
Ísafjarðardjúp
Hornstrandir
Fökulfirðir
Drangajökull
Siglufjö

Bolungarvik
Suðureyri
Flateyri
Ísafjördur
Dynjandifoss
Súðavík
Skagafjörður
Þingeyri
Arnarfjördur
Hrafnseyri
Gláma
Húnaflói
Saudarkrókur
Bildudalur
Tálknafjördur
Hólmavík
Drangsnes
Blönduós
Glaumbær
Patreksfjördur
Varmahlið
Látrabjarg
Brjánslækur
Viðimyri
Flatey
Reykhólar
670m
Hvammstangi
Rjúpnafell
Breidafjördur
Laugarbakki
Hvammsfjörður
Stykkishólmur
Búdardalur
Ólafsvík
Grundarfjördur
Hellisdandur
Snæfellsnes
Snæfellsjökull
Tröllakirkja
Hella
Surtshellir
Hve
Malarrif
Arnarstapi
Langjökull
Kjölu
Snorri's
Pool
Húsafell
Svignaskard
Kaldidalur
Kerl
ff
1204m
Reykholt
Blafell
Borgarnes
149
Faxaflói
Akranes
Hvalfjörður
Geysir & Strokkur
Gullfoss
Viðey
Þingvellir
Thingvallavatn
Þjó
REYKJAVÍK
Kópavogur
Laugarvatn
803m
Hengill
Skálholt
Keflavík
Hafnarfjördur
Hek
Hafnir
R e y k j a n e s
Hveragerdi
Landmannala
Blá Lónid
Krýsuvík
Selfoss
Grindavík
Thorlákshöfn
Hella
Þórsmörk
Hvolsvöllur
Fljótsdalur
Eyjafjalla-
Jökull
Skó
Vestmannaeyjar
Heimaey
Surtsey
D

A   B   C

4

3

2

1

Grímsey

Raufarhöfn

Kópasker

Thistilfjördur

Öxarfjördur

Lundey

Bakkaflói

Thórshöfn

lafsfjördur

Halbjarnastadir

Skjálfandi

Bakkafjördur

Grenivik

Húsavik

■ Ásbyrgi

Vopnafjördur

alvík

■ Jökulsárgljúfur

■ Dettifoss

Vopnafjördur

Héradsflói

Reykjahlid

Grimsstadir

kureyri Godafoss

Skjálfandafljót

Borgarfjördur
Eystri

Myvatn

Eidar

Seydisfjördur

Eyjafjardardalur

Saurbær

1222m
Bláfjall

Mödrudalur

Jökulsá á Fjöllum

Egilsstadir **Neskaupstadur**

Myri

Lagarfljót

1682m
Herdubreid

Hallormsstadur

Eskifjördur

Ódádahraun

■ Askja

Jökulsá á Brú

Reydarfjördur

Faskrúdsfjördur

Laugafell

Dyngjufjöll

Öskjuvatn

Stödvarfjördur

Sprengisandur

Breiddalsvik

1833m
▲ Snæfell

Thrandar-
jökull

Berufjördur

jökull *Tungnafells-*
jökull

Dyngjujökull

1920m
▲ Kverkfjöll

Brúarjökull

Djúpivogur

Vatnajökull

Grímsvötn ■

Skálafellsjökull

órisvatn

Sidujökull

Skeidarárjökull

Höfn

Lónsvik

Stokksnes

818m
Laki

Skaftafell ■

■ Jökulsárlón

Eldgjá

■ Öræfajökull
▲ *2119m*
Hvannadalshnúkur

Skeidarársandur

Kirkjubæjarklaustur

| 0 | 50 | 100 km |

D E F

The West

This area encompasses a little of just about eveything Iceland has to offer, from the two west-pointing prongs that are the majestic Snæfellsnes mountain ridge and flatter lava-flow of the Reykjanes peninsula, to the coxcomb of the deeply indented older rock of the West Fjords which form the northwest tip of Europe. To the south, the fertile floodplain of the Ölfusá and Thjórsa rivers marks one end of the great geological rift which splits Iceland in two and spat up the Westmann Islands. The early settlers made their home here and there are important centres of history at Thingvellir, Reykholt and of course, the capital, Reykjavík.

> *'Reykjavík… is a fishy town. Along the unoccupied parts of the street, or the shore, at every little bit of vantage ground which could be found vacant, there were fishes laid out to dry.'*

ANTHONY TROLLOPE,
How the 'Mastiffs' went to Iceland
(1878)

———————•———————

The city's old wooden houses are faced with corrugated iron

ℹ www.tourist.reykjavik.is

Reykjavík

Iceland's capital city is pleasingly unique. Its colourful old painted buildings of wood and tin in the haphazard streets around the old harbour give it the appearance of a frontier town, and are a reminder that Reykjavík barely appeared on the map before the end of the 18th century. It has no grand buildings like other European capitals, for Iceland was a poor country before the last century.

But the unsophisticated, homely feel is deceptive: the locals publish and read more books per head than anywhere else in the world; and they embrace new technological gadgetry with an enthusiasm that borders on the obsessive and leaves bigger, more entrenched countries of Europe lumbering in their wake. Paradoxically, they work long hours and hard (often with extra summer jobs) to maintain an admirably high standard of living; yet they retain a broad world view and a laid-back attitude to life, a healthy resistance to authority, a sense of fun and mischief; they drink to get drunk and are sentimental about a country small enough to behave like a community.

There's plenty to ⬚⬚⬚⬚⬚ ⬚ a short break, with surprisingly go⬚ ⬚⬚⬚ ⬚⬚⬚ent restaurants and lots of good small ⬚⬚ ⬚⬚⬚⬚eries to explore which are dominated b⬚ ⬚⬚⬚ ⬚⬚. The famous nightlife kicks off on a Fri⬚ ⬚⬚⬚ ⬚round 11PM and nobody goes home befo⬚ ⬚⬚⬚

Tempe⬚⬚⬚ ⬚⬚ ⬚ally mild – around freezing point

*Making the most of
summer in Austurvöllur
square*

in winter, 11°C in summer. In the clear, constant light of a
summer's evening Reykjavík's a fascinating place. On a
snowy winter's night, with candlelight glowing through
every window, it's enchanting.

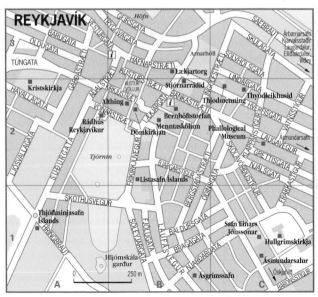

✚ 29A1
⊠ Kistuhylur 4
☎ 577 1111;
www.arbaejarsafn.is
🕐 Jun–Aug, Tue–Fri 10–5,
Sat–Sun 10–6; regular
afternoon tours in winter
🚌 110 from Lækjartorg, 10
from Hlemmur
♿ None
🍴 Cheap
❓ Look for demonstration
and craft days. Milking
takes place at 4:30 every
day. Guided tours in
winter Mon, Wed, Fri 1–2

*Turf walls and roof
insulate a traditional
old house by the church
at Árbær*

✚ 29C2
⊠ Sigtun
☎ 553 2155
🕐 May–Sep, daily 10–4;
Oct–Apr, daily 1–4
🚌 5 from Lækjartorg and
Hlemmur
♿ None 🍴 Cheap
↔ See his sculpture of a
milkmaid at Árbæjarsafn
(► above)
❓ Part of Reykjavík Art
Museum

What to See in Reykjavík

ÁRBÆJARSAFN
(REYKJAVÍK CITY MUSEUM)

For a glimpse into lives of the past, this open-air museum site is nosy-parkers' heaven. Since 1957 interesting old houses have been migrating – lock, stock and barrel – from the centre of Reykjavík to form a unique historical collection to the east of the city. The original farmstead of Árbær, with its turf roof, has been joined by buildings of timber, stone and iron-cladding from all across Iceland. The church, which was brought here from Skagafjörður, dates from 1842 and is a picturesque spot for summer wedding parties. You can go into many of the houses to enjoy the period furnishings; often you feel that the real owner has just slipped into the next room. Traditional craft days bring the old skills to life – join in the haymaking and butter-churning and watch the blacksmith at work.

ÁSMUNDARSAFN (ÁSMUNDUR   ✪
SVEINSSON SCULPTURE GALLERY)

The extraordinary whitewashed building with its golf-ball dome, likened to an igloo, was designed and built in the 1940s by the artist as his home and studio. It's now a museum to him, but his work is at its most impressive in the outdoor sculpture garden. Sveinsson (1893–1982) studied in Copenhagen and Paris and became one of Iceland's leading popular sculptors. He took his inspiration from the sagas, nature and the oddities of people in everyday life, and his abstract work explores a variety of styles. You'll recognise his distinctively bold and primitive forms everywhere.

Austurvöllur is the old heart of the city, and a lively meeting place in summer

AUSTURVÖLLUR ✪✪

This peaceful leafy square, surrounded by shops and restaurants, lies at the heart of the old town on the site where Ingólfur Arnarson, the man known as the First Settler, had his hay meadows – the name means 'east field'. Given this historical provenance, it is entirely appropriate that the modest grey stone Althingishús (parliament building) of 1881 should form the southern side. Some 63 MPs meet in the modern building next door from Monday to Thursday, with a Prime Minister and an elected president at their head. The statue in the centre of the square is of Jón Sigurðsson (1811–79), hero of the call for independence from Denmark in 1855; in his honour, National (Independence) Day is celebrated on 17 June, his birthday. The elegant little Dómkirkjan with its square tower is the Lutheran cathedral, built in 1796. Hótel Borg, along the east side, is Iceland's oldest and most splendid hotel.

🞣 29B2
✉ Between Kirkjustræti, Vallarstræti and Pósthússtræti
🍴 Cafés and restaurants (£–£££). Try a window seat in the Café Paris for a great view of the square
↔ Walk between the Dómkirkjan and parliament building to reach the Tjörn (➤ 37)

BERNHÖFTSTORFAN ✪

A cluster of some of Reykjavík's oldest surviving buildings provides a charming centre for one of the city's three main tourist offices and the Lækjarbrekka restaurant. Dating from the end of the 18th century, this is an appealing group of wooden houses with Lækjartorg square just below. To the right down broad Lækjargata is an imposing white building with a flagpole. This is Government House (Stjórnarraðið), built in 1765. Formerly a prison workhouse, it now provides offices for the Prime Minister. On the little hill beside it stands a dramatic statue by Einar Jónsson (➤ 35) of Ingólfur Arnarson, the First Settler. To the left, the old grammar school was the first of its kind in Iceland, and lists Halldór Laxness (➤ 10) among former pupils.

🞣 29B2
✉ Tourist Information Centre, Bankastræti 2
☎ 562 3045
🕐 15 May–15 Sep, daily 8:30AM–7PM; winter Mon–Sat 9–5
🍴 Lækjarbrekka (£–£££)

ELLIÐAÁRDALUR

Iceland prides itself on its policies of clean energy sources and conservation, both of which come together very successfully in this green valley lined with trees to the east of the city centre. It's a great place to escape the traffic, with a network of footpaths and cycle tracks. Running through its heart is the sparkling and unpolluted Elliðaá, site of Iceland's first hydroelectric power station and one of the best rivers for salmon in the country – rightly a source of national pride. It's the focus of the traditional opening of the fishing season on 1 May, and you can see the salmon spawning in early August.

HALLGRÍMSKIRKJA (► 16, TOP TEN)

HÖFN (OLD HARBOUR)

You might expect to find Reykjavík's harbour along Hafnarstræti ('harbour street'), but through the 20th century the boundaries were pushed seawards and the land extended artificially to provide more space, first to Tryggvagata and now Geirsgata. You can enjoy a stroll along here and watch the fishing boats offloading in the western end, perhaps admire a cruise liner or two in the eastern end, or just sit and watch the busy world go by. A replica wooden Viking ship can often be seen here, dwarfed by the grey-painted vessels of the coastguard. Don't miss the weekend fleamarket, **KOLAPORTIÐ**, in the old Tollhús building with its beautiful mosaic wall on Tryggvagata. The market is full of bric-à-brac and clothing, with an excellent little food section selling fish and local delicacies.

KJARVALSSTAÐIR (KJARVAL COLLECTION) ✪

The art gallery, in Miklatún Park, is primarily home to a collection of surreal landscapes by Iceland's most famous artist, Jóhannes S Kjarval (1885–1972). Kjarval began his working life as a trawlerman but his skills as a painter were quickly recognised by his colleagues, who together raised the funds necessary for his study abroad, in London and Copenhagen. Stand back a little from the paintings for the best effect.

✚ 29C3
🚌 3, 4, 6, 7, 9, 10, 11, 12, 14, 15, 110, 111, 112, 115
♿ None
💷 Free

✚ 29B3
🚌 2, 3, 4, 5, 6, 7, 110, 112, 115
❓ Annual Festival of the Sea celebrated in the old harbour

KOLAPORTIÐ
✉ Geirsgata
☎ 562 5030
🕐 Sat–Sun 11–5
🍴 Café great for coffee and sandwiches (£)

Huge fishing vessels can dock near the city centre in the old harbour

---

✚ 29A1
✉ Flókagata
☎ 552 6131
🕐 Thu–Tue 10–5, Wed 10–7
🚌 3 from Lækjartorg
♿ Few
💷 Cheap
❓ Part of Reykjavík Art Museum

LAUGARDALUR ⊕⊕

Within walking distance of downtown Reykjavík; this is the city's main sports and recreation ground and it buzzes with families at weekends. The football stadium is here, as well as a fabulous outdoor **SWIMMING POOL** complete with waterslide, whirlpool and 'hot-pots' (geothermally heated, of course). For children, there's all the fun of the Norse and Viking-themed Park and Reykjavík Zoo (➤ 81), where you can stroke Icelandic horses and encounter other friendly beasts including seals and reindeer. This is also the home of the **BOTANIC GARDENS**, proof that Iceland's short growing season, unfriendly climate and volcanic soil are no obstacle to a wide range of plants and trees. Enjoy a picnic in the elegant heated pavilion.

LISTASAFN ÍSLANDS (NATIONAL GALLERY) ⊕

This tall white building with its high arched-eyebrow windows overlooks the Tjörn (➤ 37) and was originally a storage place for ice, cut from the pond and kept for use in the preservation of fish. It has been tastefully renovated in a light and modern style with lots of glass and wood-block floors, to house the national collection of paintings and sculpture, which mostly date from the 20th century and include works by artists such as Nina Tryggvadóttir. With only four rooms it's not the biggest display gallery but the exhibitions change regularly and so it's well worth a look in.

🔟 29C3
🚌 2, 5, 10, 12, 15

SWIMMING POOL
🕐 Apr–Sep, Sat and Sun 8–8;
Oct–Mar, Mon–Fri
6:50AM–9:30PM

BOTANIC GARDENS
🕐 Greenhouse and
pavilion Apr–Sep10–10;
Oct–Mar 10–5

Above: *modern art on dispaly at the National Gallery*

🔟 29B2
✉ Frikirkjuvegur 7
☎ 515 9610;
www.listasafn.is
🕐 Tue–Sun 11–5
🍴 Café (£) on upper floor for coffee and cakes
🚌 2, 3, 4, 5, 6, 7, 110, 111, 112, 115
♿ Excellent
🎟 Cheap, free Wed
↔ Opposite the Tjörn, (➤ 37)
❓ Occasional concerts held in the foyer, check locally for details. Viewpoint gallery in the basement highlights younger artists

A football-playing sculpture in the garden of the National Gallery

Town centre/shore

Distance
3km

Time
Allow at least half a day,
longer to explore properly

Sart/end point
Hallgrímskirkja
 29C1
from Lækjartorg
2,3,4,5,6,7, every 30
minutes in summer

Lunch
Café Sólon (£)
✉ Bankastræti 7A
☎ 562 3232

From the statue of Leif the Lucky (► 10), head down Skólavörðustígur.

This is an interesting street with lots of intriguing crafts galleries and jewellers, as well as the little stone gaol.

Bear right down Klapparstígur, and turn right at the bottom onto Laugavegur.

This is Reykjavík's main shopping street, full of boutiques and, increasingly, bars.

Turn left onto Frakkastígur, with views up to the Hallgrímskirkja and down to the steel Viking ship sculpture, Sólfar by Jón Gunnar Árnason (1931–89). At the bottom of the hill cross the busy road and turn left to follow the harbour path.

There are great views across the bay and to Mount Esja, with the harbour ahead.

Keep right past the harpoon-head sculpture and continue with the fishing harbour opening out on your right to the sculpture of two fishermen. Turn right here and continue along the harbour, then bear left into Tryggvagata, which hooks you back towards the town centre. Turn right into the square, passing the Tourist Information Centre (toilets up to your right, free).

There are lots of bars and restaurants around this popular downtown area.

Keep right and turn up Aðalstræti, passing some of the city's oldest houses on your right. Pass the old well and pump, and turn left across a paved square to enter Austurvöllur square. Pass the old parliament building on your right, and go stright on, to turn left onto Lækjargata towards the harbour. Turn right up Bankastræti, and bear diagonally right up Skólavörðustígur to return to the Hallgrímskirkja.

Harpoon sculpture by the old harbour

ÖSKJUHLÍÐ ⭐⭐⭐

A massive space-age edifice squats on Öskjuhlíð hill, to the south of town. Its great towers hold 18 million litres of geothermally heated water – enough to service half the city. Between them is an exhibition space on different levels, with a café, and a mini-geyser which shoots up from the basement. The jewel in this crown is definitely on the top, however – the reflective glass dome is actually one of Reykjavík's most exclusive dining palaces, Perlan, The Pearl. The restaurant rotates as you eat but don't worry about spilling your soup – one complete revolution takes two hours. Food with a view comes at a price, but you can go out on the balconies for free and see across to Mount Esja. The new Saga Museum in one of the towers presents the history of Viking settlement in Iceland.

🞢 29A1
✉ Perlan, Öskjuhlíð
☎ 562 0200
🕐 Open daily
🍴 Café (£); Perlan restaurant (£££)
🚌 7
♿ Excellent
👋 Free

The glass dome of The Pearl rotates on top of the city's hot water tanks

PHALLOLOGICAL MUSEUM ⭐

A bit of an oddity, but offering a different sort of exhibition for a wet afternoon, the museum houses a collection of some 150 preserved animal penises.

🞢 29C2
✉ Laugavegur 24
☎ 561 6663
🕐 May–Aug, Tue–Sat 2–5; Sep–Apr, Thu– Sat 2–5

SAFN EINARS JÓNSSONAR ⭐⭐⭐
(EINAR JÓNSSON SCULPTURE MUSEUM)

High on the top of Skólavörðuholt hill, Iceland's outstanding sculptor Einar Jónsson (1874–1954) built his fortress-like house and gallery. The outside may be forbidding but inside is a collection of fantastical sculpted figures which demonstrate the extraordinary imagination of the artist. Mythical creatures of gigantic proportions emerge from the living rocks of the Icelandic landscape, or swoop up from the seas in breathtaking beauty. Look out for the terrifying troll figure, petrified in the sunrise, the teeth in his skull-like face already becoming basalt columns; and the famous *Outlaws* statue, inspiration for one of Halldór Laxness's oddest heroes, Bjartur of Summerhouses (▶ 10). The sculptures carry on below and into the garden, and you can explore the artist's living quarters at the top of narrow spiral stairs.

🞢 29C1
✉ Eiríksgata
☎ 551 3797
🕐 Jun–Sep, Tue–Sun 2–5; Sep–May, Sat–Sun 2–5; closed Dec–Jan. Sculpture garden open all year, access from Freyjugata
🚌 7
♿ None
👋 Cheap; sculpture garden free
↔ Opposite the Hallgrímskirkja (▶ 16)
❓ Labels in Icelandic only; ask at the ticket desk for an invaluable sheet of translations

35

🪑 29C2
✉ Hverfisgata 15
☎ 545 1400;
www.thjodmenning.is
🕐 Daily 11–5
🍴 Café on ground floor (£)
♿ Good
🎙 Cheap
❓ Permanent displays of
manuscripts and maps
are augmented
by changing
exhibitions on
the top floor

THJOÐMENNING (CULTURE HOUSE) ⭐⭐

Iceland is unique in having a written culture that goes back to its earliest days. The language, akin to Old Norse, has hardly changed over the last 1,000 years, and so the literature can be read as easily by people today as when it was written. The Sagas, complex and lively medieval tales of history, landscape, lineage and epic deeds, are still very much alive and at the heart of Icelandic culture, and this is the best place to learn more of their story. The

An ornamental capital adorns a 14th-century manuscript

manuscripts survive in books and fragments of vellum, gathered up by one man, Árni Magnússon, in the period 1702–12. They were transported to Denmark for study but unfortunately many were destroyed in the Great Fire of Copenhagen in 1728. The best were rescued, however, and in 1971 the first of these were ceremoniously returned to their homeland, including *Landnámabók*, *Íslandingabók*, and *Njál's Saga*. Look out for the tiny wood-bound *Margaret's Saga*.

DID YOU KNOW?

That the sagas and other books were originally copied out on vellum, or calf skin. One calf skin would make just two pages, and many manuscripts ran to 200 pages and more.

THJÓÐMINJASAFN ✪✪✪
ÍSLANDS
(NATIONAL MUSEUM)

This is the place to see the tangible signs of the earliest Viking settlement of Iceland, from tools dating from the Settlement era, to religious and folk relics. Archaeological finds from all over the country are housed under one roof, giving an important insight into Icelandic history.

🔲 29A1
✉ Suðurgata 41
☎ 530 2200;
   www.natmus.is
🕓 Check details locally – closed for renovation until April 2004

Feeding the ducks and geese on Tjörnin, overlooked by the City Hall

TJÖRNIN ✪✪✪

Of all Reykjavik's open spaces the area around the Tjörn, or pond, is one of the most fun. Some 40 species of birds breed here, despite its city-centre location, and on most days the sound of ducks, geese and swans waiting to be fed will lead you straight to it. A walkway runs below the main road (Fríkirkjuvegur) offering good views of the old houses opposite. The big grey building at the northern end is the controversial City Hall – inside there's a tourist information desk and an exhibition area used mainly for photography and art. Locals say the best view of the lake is from the coffee shop – because you can't see the ugly modern lines of the City Hall itself.

🔲 29A2
🚌 2, 3, 4, 5, 6, 7, 110, 111, 112, 115
✉ Tourist Information, City Hall
☎ 563 2005
🕓 Mon–Fri 8:20–4:30, Sat noon–6PM; also Sun noon–6PM May–Sep
🍴 Café in City Hall (£)
♿ Few
🆓 Free
↔ National Gallery (Listasafn Íslands ➤ 33) overlooks Tjörnin

VIÐEY ✪✪✪

The citizens of Reykjavík come to this romantic island to get away from it all. Low-lying and green, it's ten minutes off shore and easily explored in a day. The island boasts a top restaurant too — you can come out just for the evening and be ferried home again at the end of your meal.

There was once a monastery here and the island is full of history. Around 1755 entrepreneur and Royal Superintendent Skúli Magnússon had a stone house built as a sign of wealth and confidence (the oldest original building in Iceland, now restored to hold the restaurant); his attempts to turn the fortunes of Reykjavík failed and he died bankrupt in 1794 – there's a memorial to him by the church. A small community made the island their home in the last century, centring their hopes on a fishery, but it too failed and now the village is deserted.

🔲 29C3
✉ Kollafjörður
🍴 Viðeyjarstofa ☎ 562 1934: afternoon coffee and cake, restaurant (booking essential)
⛴ Ferry from Sundahöfn, ☎ 5811010/892 0099 for information and booking
♿ None
❓ Can be combined on a half-day trip with a visit to the puffin island of Lundey

YLSTRÖDIN NAUTHÓLSVÍK ✪

Golden sands and coastal swimming are not what you expect to find in Iceland. But here, in the shadow of Reykjavík airport, a facility offering just that opened in 2000. The sand comes from Skaftafell and the water is geothermally heated to 19–20˚ C in the lagoon.

🔲
✉ South of Öskjuhlíð
☎ 511 6630
🕓 May–Sep 10–10
🆓 Free, but small charge for use of changing rooms

What to See in the West

ARNARSTAPI ✪✪✪

The delightful cove of Arnarstapi is perfectly set on the end of the great Snæfellsnes peninsula, its steep cliffs and stacks home to a myriad of screaming sea birds, its wooden holiday cottages all turned to face the view and the sunshine. As you turn down towards the sheltered harbour, you can't miss the gigantic boulderous, be-hatted figure on the clifftop to your right. He's Bárður Snæfellsás, a spirit who lives in the great mountain of Snæfellsjökull which shelters the village to the north. The cliffs are riddled with blow-holes and echoing caves and, to the west, there's a natural stone arch. The coastline is a nature reserve, and from the car park above the harbour you can take the footpath to neighbouring Hellnar. A small community of New Age enthusiasts live here, attracted by the supposed magic properties of the mountain.

BLÁA LÓNIÐ (BLUE LAGOON) ➤ 12, TOP TEN

BORGARNES ✪

Travelling northwards on Route 1 you turn a corner to see the pretty town of Borgarnes stretched out along its narrow peninsula on the opposite shore of Borgarfjörður. In its beautiful but exposed location, with the plains of Myrar behind and the mountains to the west and south, it catches all the available light and sunshine. This is Iceland's biggest non-fishing town. A little white church with a dark-hatted

---

✚ 24A3

✉ On southwest end of Snæfellsnes peninsula, Route 574

🍴 Snjófell restaurant at Arnarstapi (£–££); excellent summer café on the beach at Hellnar (£)

Boat trips and whale-watching from Ólafsvík, contact Sæferðir-Eyjaferðir ☎ 438 1450

↔ Snæfellsjökull (➤ 46)

❓ For cycle hire, snowmobiling and camping contact Snjófell, Arnarstapi ☎ 435 6783

✚ 24B2

✉ On Route 1, 74km north of Reykjavik

📞 Tourist Information Centre at Hyran service centre ☎ 437 2214

🍴 Hótel Borgarnes (££)

🚌 All the Reykjavik buses pass through here on their way to the West fjords or Akureyri

With its church set high on the rocky peninsula, Borgarnes was founded in 1858

steeple dominates the skyline, giving it an unexpectedly Alpine air. There are strong connections in this area with *Egil's Saga*, and Egil's father Skallagrímur was buried in the town's triangle of green park, with his horse and other accoutrements as befitted a great chief. The relief depicts Egil himself, carrying the body of his son Böðvar, who drowned near by. The farm and church at Borg á Mýrum, just north of Borgarnes, mark the spot where the body of Egil's grandfather, Kveldúlfur, was washed ashore in its coffin, setting a good omen for his settler family.

Far left: *sea birds nest in their thousands around the steep stacks at Arnarstapi*

BÚÐARDALUR ✪

This unassuming farming community at the head of Hvammsfjörður marks the gateway to Laxárdalur – the salmon river valley and setting for Iceland's most romantic *Laxdæla Saga*. The tale is set around the tragic love of two foster brothers, Kjartan and Bolli, for lovely Guðrun Ósvífurs-dóttir, who was born up the coast at Laugar around AD 973. She is commemorated at the **FOLK MUSEUM** in Dalir.

➕ 24B3
✉ On Route 60, 154km north of Reykjavik

FOLK MUSEUM
✉ Laugar, Dalasýsla
☎ 434 1328
🕙 Jun–Aug, daily 9–6
💰 Cheap

FLATEY (➤ 13, TOP TEN)

GULLFOSS & GEYSIR (➤ 14–15, TOP TEN)

HAFNARFJÖRÐUR ✪✪

Overshadowed by neighbouring Reykjavík, Hafnarfjörður has always boasted a better natural harbour and has been a busy fishing port for over 60 years. It hosts the Hafnarfjörður Museum, but is perhaps best known locally as the town which takes elves seriously. So seriously, in fact, that roads have been diverted to avoid upsetting the little people. Thanks to the work of a local seer, there's now a 'Hidden World' map available at the tourist information centre showing pixie hot-spots around the town.

Hafnarfjörður is also the centre for modern Viking activities, offering an imaginative Viking-themed restaurant, Fjörukráin, in a magnificent old wooden house down by the harbour. This is the focus for the riotous activities of the international Viking Festivals, and some pretty lively behaviour on Friday and Saturday nights too.

➕ 24B2
🍴 Full range of cafés and restaurants (£–£££)
ℹ Vesturgata 8 ☎ 565 0661; www.lava.is
🕙 May–Sep, Mon–Fri 9–6, Sat, Sun 9–2; Sep–May, Mon–Fri 1–4
🚢 Short and long sea trips available, including whale-watching and sea-angling
❓ International Viking Festival about every two years, last held 2003
☎ 565 1213

Hafnarfjörður has become the Viking capital of Iceland

+ 24B2
⛴ Whale-spotting trips from Sandgerði **☎** 421 7777
ℹ Tjarnargötu 2, Reykjanesbær **☎** 421 6700

SÆFISKASAFNIÐ (AQUARIUM)
☎ 421 6958
🕐 All year 2–4
♿ None **🏷** Cheap

+ 24A3
⊠ On Route 574, 245km northwest of Reykjavík
↔ Snæfellsjökull (**➤** 46)

SJÓMANNAGARÐURINN VIÐ ÚTNESVEG (MUSEUM)
⊠ Útnesvegur
☎ 436 6961
🕐 Jun–Sep, Tue–Sun 1–6
♿ None
🏷 Cheap

+ 24C2

HAFNIR ☺☺

The Reykjanes peninsula marks the southwestern end of the great geological fault which runs diagonally across the country. On its furthest tip is the scattered former fishing village of Hafnir. You can discover more about Iceland's piscatorial heritage at the fascinating AQUARIUM, well stocked with local sea and freshwater fish. Look out for the anchor of the ghost ship *Jamestown*; abandoned off the coast of America in 1867, it drifted ashore here three years later, complete with its cargo of timber. To the south, the rocks swarm with migrant and nesting birds, including gannets from the offshore island of Eldey.

HELLISSANDUR ☺

Set on the northwestern tip of the Snæfellsnes peninsula, on the edge of the black lava field that flows down from Snæfellsjökull, this town has spectacular views to the cliffs of the West Fjords. At the MUSEUM you can explore an old fisherman's hut and boat, and there are lots of paths and tracks to follow amid the lava. Hellissandur's biggest claim to fame is the towering radio mast, 412m high, which was the tallest structure in Europe when it was built in 1959. In such a windy place, the mast would have snapped off had it been dug into the ground, so instead it is balanced on a point and held up by wires. Spare a thought for the two people (one a woman) who keep its paintwork fresh.

HEKLA ☺☺☺

The country's most infamous – and still very active – volcano last erupted in March 2000, and Icelanders are holding their breath waiting for the big one. It is known to erupt about every 10 years, with the last major eruption in 1991, but scientists suspect that recent rumblings may

herald a new period of activity. The volcano forms a ridged mountain 1,491m high on the great geological rift which divides Iceland, looming over the lowlands of the southwest with its top usually hidden modestly away in cloud. In the Middle Ages it was notorious throughout Europe as the gateway to hell. Visit the newly refurbished **HEKLA CENTRE** to learn more.

HORNSTRANDIR

Hornstrandir has always been remote and isolated; in the days when people lived on its fjords the only way in or out was by sea, and it's the same today. Its high barren uplands, lush lowlands and rugged cliffs are protected now as a nature reserve, and the banning of sheep as well as vehicles has meant a return of the land to meadow and wildflowers. To reach this hiker's paradise, catch the boat from Ísafjörður, making sure you have everything you need with you for several days – there's no accommodation other than emergency huts and the odd summer house, and you must be prepared for every sort of weather. You'll be rewarded by peace and, with luck, an abundance of wildlife, including Arctic foxes.

HÚSAFELL

This beautiful spot near the head of a long valley is covered in low birch trees and littered with gaily painted summer houses, testament to its warm temperatures and handy supply of natural hot water. A popular centre for camping, it is set about with attractive wilderness and icecaps, notably Eiríksjökull, Langjökull and Ok. You can take the high road over to Kaldidalur or hike from the valley head to explore the lava caves – the longest, Kalmanshellir, is 4km.

HEKLA CENTRE (AUDIO-VISUAL EXPLANATIONS)

✉ Brúarlandur, off Route 26
☎ 487 6591
🕐 All year (ring for opening times)
♿ None
💰 Cheap

➕ 24B4
✉ Northern tip of West Fjords, access on foot or by boat only
🚢 Scenic boat trips and tours from Ísafjörður
ℹ Aðalstræti 7, Ísafjörður
☎ 456 5121/5111

➕ 24C2
✉ On Route 518, east of Reykholt
☎ 435 1550 (accommodation)
🍴 Snack bar (£–££)
🚌 Daily bus in summer from Reykjavík via Thingvellir and Kaldidalur
➤ See also drive (➤ 43), Reykholt (➤ 45)
❓ Guided walks to the caves ☎ 435 1558

Hekla, still covered in snow, broods while summer flowers carpet the older lava fields

➕ 24B2
✉️ 43km north of Reykjavík
🔁 See drive (➤ 43)

BYGGÐASAFNIÐ Í GÖRÐUM (FOLK MUSEUM)

✉️ Garður, by Akranes
☎️ 431 1255;
www.museum.is
🕐 May–Sep, daily 10–6;
Sep–Apr, Mon–Fri 1–6
🍴 Restaurant in the Museum Hall
✋ Moderate

HVALFJÖRÐUR ⭐⭐

It is said that you may see up to 17 species of whale in this deep fjord during late summer. The whales were particularly welcomed in days gone by – you can see something of the history of local whaling (ended in 1989) and 'Cod Wars' at the excellent Garður **FOLK MUSEUM**. This narrow finger of water is sheltered by Mount Esja to the south and Skarðsheiði to the north and, now that it has been bypassed by the tunnel at Saurbær, it has returned to something like tranquility, with only the ferro-silicon smelter on the northern shore to mar its beauty. Irish monks were the first settlers here, commemorated by a stone in the cemetery at Akranes. It's difficult to imagine this peaceful place bristling with naval hardware, but during World War II the Allies had a massive base here and it was a key location for the North Atlantic convoys.

➕ 24B2
✉️ On Route 1, 38km southeast of Reykjavík
🍴 Café with pastries to die for at Hverabakarí (bakery), Breiðamörk 10
ℹ️ South Iceland Information Centre, Breiðamörk 2
☎️ 483 4601;
www.hveragerdi.is

Above: a humpback whale cuts through the water

HVERAGERÐI ⭐

You'll notice that there are no tower blocks in this town – it's built on the edge of an active geothermal area and small earthquakes are commonplace. Steam from the naturally hot water (reaching 200°C underground) is used to heat greenhouses – pause at Eden for souvenirs and a taste of tropical plantlife. There's good walking in the hills, and a geothermal area in the town centre with boiling mud pots and sulphurous fumaroles. You could even treat yourself to a mud bath at the health spa. One spring is named Ruslahver, or 'garbage hot spring', after the rubbish that had been tipped down it when it was a dry hole was spewed back up during an earthquake.

Rekjavík to Húsafell

Explore small towns, a beautiful long valley and a spectacular fjord.

Take Route 1 north from Reykjavík, via Mosfellsbær. At Hvalfjörður follow signs for the tunnel (toll payable). At the other side, turn left onto Route 51 to Akranes. Turn off before Akranes on the 503 for Garður museum (➤ 42). Head north on Route 51. Turn left and left again, and follow Route 1 to Borgarnes (➤ 38).

To the left, the fertile plains are dotted with farms; to your right are sweeping fells of black scree, giving way to bushy vegetation.

Cross the scenic causeway to Borgarnes and stay on Route 1 towards Akureyri.

This beautiful wide valley is a popular holiday spot, with marked walking trails. Great viewpoint at Svignaskarð.

Turn right at the octagonal service station, Baulan, on Route 50 to Reykholt. Stay on this road, signed to Reykjavík, then bear left towards Reykholt on the 518, reached after 5km.

Explore the church, museum centre and Snorri's pool (➤ 45). The Hótel Reykholt is just behind.

Continue on Route 518 to Húsafell (➤ 41), passing the lovely Hraunfossar waterfalls on your left. Stay on the 518 around the head of the valley. At Brúará bridge, stay on the 523 to pass a café at Bjarnastaðir; at the junction with the 522 turn left, and right onto Route 50 to Borgarnes. Turn left onto Route 1 and retrace route south to the junction with Route 47. Turn left here for Hvalfjörður (➤ 42) and take the old road around this fabulous fjord. Rejoin Route 1 and return to Reykjavík.

Distance
300km

Time
Allow a full day, or take it slowly and spread over two

Start/end point
A circular route from Reykjavík
🔲 24B2

Lunch
Hótel Reykholt (££)

Summer camps dot the landscape at Húsafell

43

HVOLSVÖLLUR ✪✪

🚩 24C1
✉ 106km southeast of Reykjavik

**SÖGUSETRIÐ
(SAGA CENTRE)**
☎ 487 8781
🕐 Jun–Aug, daily 9–5
🍴 Hlíðarendi restaurant by petrol station (£–££)
♿ None
💷 Cheap
❓ Musical presentation in various languages Jul–Aug, 7PM. Advance booking essential

In the flat, fertile land north of the Thverá river lies the village of Hvolsvöllur, all too easily bypassed by the hurrying tourist anxious for the next great sight. Instead, pause awhile, for you are entering the magical country of one of the greatest of epics, Njál's Saga, and the **SAGA**

CENTRE here will help you to make sense of it all. As well as exhibitions explaining the characters, the story and its locations, the centre sets this best-loved Saga in the context of the Viking age. Story telling was once a fundamental part of Icelandic life and here the art is revived in a specially recreated medieval hall.

ÍSAFJÖRÐUR ✪✪

🚩 24B4
✉ 457km north of Reykjavík
ℹ Aðalstræti 7 ☎ 456 5121
🕐 Mon–Fri 8–6, and summer weekends 10–3

Above: *learn more of the saga of Burnt Njál*

Dramatically set on its own inlet of the wide Ísafjarðarjúp fjord and sheltered by mountains, Ísafjörður is the capital of the remote West Fjords region. It is the jumping-off point for a wide range of activities including mini-cruises, whale-watching, hiking and sea-angling in summer, and skiing in winter, and is also the gateway to Hornstrandir (➤ 41). The town was one of Iceland's key trading ports from 1569 to the early 19th century, and a complex of four old wooden houses on the seafront bears testament to this. Cod, shark and herring were all sought with *thilskip* (small boats with decks) instead of the more common open rowing boats.

KRÝSUVÍK ✪

🚩 24B1
✉ South of Reykjavík on Route 42
🔄 Sometimes combined on a tour with the Blue Lagoon (➤ 12)

If you've only got a short time to visit Iceland, then this is the most interesting geothermal site near Reykjavík where you can stroll among smelly steam holes and horribly bubbling mud pools – it's no surprise to learn that sulphur was once mined here. The gloriously multi-coloured volcanic scoria beneath your feet can be hot and uncertain, so be careful where you tread and stick to the boardwalks. The whole area is part of the Reykjanesfólkvangur national reserve.

DID YOU KNOW?

Iceland has around 200 volcanoes and 250 natural hot springs, and has produced about one third of the total world lava flow in the last 400 years. Almost three-quarters of the country has no permanent vegetation cover.

LÁTRABJARG ✪✪✪

Nowhere in Iceland are the sea birds so tightly packed along the cliffs as here, on the westernmost point of Europe. This older rock, in a sheer, undulating line of cliffs that stretch some 11km and rise to 511m high, has been worn and ground on its exposed seaward surface to form natural ledges, which are like high-rise penthouses to a vast density of kittiwakes and fulmars, guillimots, puffins and one-third of the world's total population of razorbills. From a distance it is like watching a swarming beehive as the birds fly up and down and out to sea, and close up the noise of their calling is incredible. In days gone by, hardy locals would lower themselves over the edge on a rope to collect the eggs in a test of bravery, skill and basic survival.

🚩 24A3
✉ Western tip of the West Fjords

REYKHOLT ✪✪

The greatest of writers Snorri Sturluson (➤ 10) lived in this beautiful rolling valley from 1206–41, composing his mighty history of Norwegian kings, *Heimskringla*. He had his own thermal bathing pool, Snorralaug, once linked straight to his farm by a tunnel, which you can see steaming beyond the church. The MODERN CENTRE FOR MEDIEVAL RESEARCH is dedicated to him – with its tall-hatted spire, it's a distinctive landmark. A statue of Snorri stands outside the former grammar school, currently being converted to a library.

🚩 24B2
✉ Turn left off Route 527, in the Hvita valley, 43km east of Borgarnes

SNORRASTOFA-HEIMSKRINGLA CENTRE (MODERN CENTRE FOR MEDIEVAL RESEARCH)
✉ 320 Reykholt
☎ 435 1490/435 1491
🕐 Jun–Aug daily, 10–6
🍴 Hótel Reykholt behind old farmstead
🚗 See drive (➤ 43)
❓ Car parks below centre and futher along main road; centre is focus of an annual music festival in July

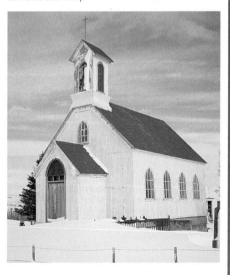

Members of Snorri's family, the Sturlungas, are buried around the old church of Reykolt

The stark lines of
Stykkishólmur church,
high above the bay

🚩 24C2
✉ Northeast of Selfoss on
Route 31, just north of
Laugarás

CHURCH
✉ Biskupstungur, 801
Selfoss
☎ 486 8870
🕐 Daily
🍴 Refreshments available in
school building
♿ None
❓ Free concerts at
weekends in Jul and Aug

🚩 24A3
✉ Western tip of
Snæfellsnes, 195km
northwest of Reykjavík
ℹ Gamla Pakkhúsið,
Ólafsvík ☎ 436 1543
🕐 Summer only
❓ Glacier trips from
Arnarstapi (➤ 38) and
Ólafsvík; winter skiing
from Ólafsvík

SKÁLHOLT ✪✪

The stark white **CHURCH** at Skálholt stands out of the green landscape like a beacon. It is only 50 years old but there have been similar buildings on this important site for centuries since one of the country's first two bishoprics was founded here in 1056. In 1550 the community was taught a sharp lesson when rebel Catholic bishop Jón Arason was summarily beheaded for opposing the introduction of Lutheranism from Denmark. Skálholt remained a (now Lutheran) bishopric until a general migration to Reykjavík at the end of the 18th century. In the church you can admire the massive stone sarcophagus of another early bishop, Páll Jónsson, and the striking modern mosaic of Christ by artist Nina Tryggvadóttir.

SNÆFELLSJÖKULL ✪✪✪

On a clear day you can see the iced pixie-hat peak of this mountain, apparently floating weightless above the sea, all the way from Reykjavík. It's not the biggest glacier in the country but one of the most appealing and accessible. Perched on the end of the long ridge of Snæfellsnes, the views from the top are fantastic. Jules Verne picked it as the gateway to the underworld in *Journey to the Centre of the Earth* (he obviously hadn't been through the Hvalfjördur tunnel), and even today it revels in a dubious mystical reputation which acts as a magnet for New Agers and free spirits. You can get to the top fairly easily from Arnarstapi or Ólafsvík by snowmobile or skidoo – make sure you stick to your guide's tracks in summer, when crevasses can be dangerous. It's a popular spot for family picnics and tobogganing.

STYKKISHÓLMUR ✪✪

This windblown town on the north shore of Snæfellsnes is an odd mixture of good, bad and plain ugly. Approaching by road, you see the sweeping white pylon 'H' of the church off to your right, a lively and daring piece of modern architecture. There are some splendid old wooden houses down by the harbour, including the black-painted Norwegian House of 1832, now a museum and gallery but built as the home of Iceland's first meteorologist, Árni Thorlacius. The old centre is dominated by the looming ochre walls of a Franciscan convent, however, which seems out of place amid the gaily painted houses. Paganism has always had a place here and to prove it there's a magical hill, Helgafell, where – if you follow the rules – you may be granted three wishes. Look out for scallop shells in the bay; the other local speciality is traditionally cured shark (*hákarl*) – follow your nose westwards to Bjarnarhöfn.

🞧 24B3
🗺 At the end of Route 58
🍴 Several restaurants and snack bars
⛴ Ferry sailings ☎ 438 1450
🛈 Borgarbraut ☎ 438 1150/1750; www.stykkisolmur.is
↔ Flatey (➤ 13)
❓ *Baldur*, the car and passenger ferry across Breiðafjörður bay to Flatey and the West Fjords, leaves here on its daily circuit. Also sightseeing cruises and whale-watching tours

THINGVELLIR (➤ 21, TOP TEN)

The mountain peak of Snæfellsjökull glows pink in the dawn light

THÓRSMÖRK ✪✪✪

One of the world's great treks, that from the extraordinary lunarscape of Landmannalaugar, leads over the mountains to this remote and beautiful nature reserve set about with birch woods, entwined rivers and superb glacier-topped scenery. It's a wilderness with its own warmer microclimate, best explored on foot. Don't expect to drive there unless you're with an experienced group – the road into the valley crosses the powerful and dangerous Krossá river, and this is best left to the experts with their specially high-set coaches.

🞧 24C1
🗺 Access up F249, off Route 1 south of Hvolsvöllur
↔ Hvolsvöllur (➤ 44); Landmannalaugar (➤ 69)

VESTMANNAEYJAR (WESTMANN ISLANDS) ➤ 22, TOP TEN

In the Know

If you have only a short time to visit Iceland, or would like to get a real flavour of the country, here are some ideas:

10
Ways to Be a Local

Think big – Icelanders love plans on a grand scale.

Eat fish – Icelandic sea fish is some of the best you'll ever taste. Try it dried for a snack.

Keep your swimming togs handy for a dip in one of the many thermally heated outdoor pools and hot-pots.

Remember it may have short legs, but size isn't everything – it's an Icelandic horse, never a pony.

Hike, cycle, ride, camp and enjoy the wilderness – Icelanders love their countryside and their solitude.

Hire a four-wheel-drive jeep and explore the back roads, but check out the local conditions first and don't take silly risks.

Avoid disturbing the wildlife and, if you must walk near ground-nesting birds, wear a hat – you may get your head pecked.

Start your party late – nobody in Reykjavík gets going before 11PM.

Don't wrinkle your nose in disgust when you turn on the hot water – after a week or so you'll stop noticing the faint whiff of sulphur.

Believe in the powers of the wee folk – some 80 per cent of Icelanders admit to a belief in elves.

10
Good Places to Have Lunch

CAFÉ PARIS (£)
 Austervöllur, Reykjavík
☎ 551 1020
Bag a window seat, or dine al fresco if the sun's shining.

CAFÉ SÓLON (£)
 Bankastræti 7A, Reykjavík
☎ 562 3232
Great for a mid-shopping snack.

DELI (£)
 Bankasæti 14, Reykjavík
☎ 551 6000
Freshly made baguettes, panini and salads – perfect for a quick and tasty lunch.

FYLGIFISKAR (£–££)
 Suðurlandsbraut 10, Rekjavík ☎ 533 1303
Just a few tables in this fabulous fish shop, open Mon–Fri (Sat in winter).

PERLAN (£–££)
 Öskjuhlíð, Reykjavík
☎ 562 0200
Fourth-floor café in the famous landmark, open all day.

SVARTA KAFFIÐ (£–££)
 Laugavegur 54, Reykjavík
☎ 551 2999
The home-made soup in a bread roll is a special winter warmer.

Above: you can relax in the outdoor pools all year round
Right: Icelandic horses are small and sure-footed, and ridden by people of all ages

Whale-watching has become a top activity, and individual whales can be recognised by their markings and scars

- *Gísli Súrsson's Saga* – clever outlaw has a fatal run of bad luck
- *Saga of Hrafnkell Freysgoði* – classic saga of leadership and power, short but perfectly formed

10
Top Birds

- Barrow's goldeneye
- Gyrfalcon
- Harlequin duck
- Icelandic wren
- Pink-footed goose
- Puffin
- Red-necked phalarope
- Snow bunting
- White-tailed sea eagle
- Whooper swan

BAUTINN (£–££)
✉ Hafnarstræti 92, Akureyri
☎ 462 1818
Unfussy, with the best hamburgers in town.

BLAA KANNAN (£)
✉ Strandgata 7, Akureyri
☎ 461 3999
Lunch in stylish surroundings – and leave room for cake.

GAMLI BAUKUR (£–££)
✉ Húsavík
☎ 464 2442
Set right on the harbour, where it's all happening.

KAFFI HORNIÐ (£–££)
✉ Hafnarbraut, Höfn
☎ 478 2600
Simple food, well cooked.

- Bird-watching
- Dolphin- and whale-spotting
- Cycling
- Sea-angling
- Fishing
- River rafting
- Winter sports

5
Top Icelandic Sagas

- *Njál's Saga* – adventures of small, wise Njál and his big, hot-headed friend
- *Egil's Saga* – violent poet with ugly face dominates all around
- *Laxdæla Saga* – romance and revenge of beautiful people

Iceland is the top summer destination for some 10 million puffins

10
Top Activities

- Swimming
- Hiking
- Horse riding

The North & Northeast

The north coast is characterised by some of the most beautiful fjordland scenery, with sweeping vistas of high mountains and fertile green valleys. It offers some of the country's best salmon fishing, whale-spotting and bird life, as well as the most spectacular geothermal area around Mývatn and more than its fair share of magnificent waterfalls. The eastern part is bleaker, with rolling brown moorland, and marshland on the northern tip. In summer there is good access to the vast empty spaces of the interior, lit up by the occasional welcome oasis of green.

> *' We didn't get to Mývatn til three o'clock and I was hungry, seedy and cross. The lake is surrounded by little craters like candle snuffers and most attractive. '*
>
> W H AUDEN & LOUIS MACNEICE,
> *Letters from Iceland* (1937)

Rich agricultural land surrounds Akureyri

🔹 25D3
✉ 389km northeast of
Reykjavík on Route 1
🍴 Range of eating places
(£–£££)
🚌 Daily coach service from
Reykjavík ☎ 462 4442;
scheduled air services
from Reykjavík with Air
Iceland ☎ 460 7000
⛴ Regular ferry service to
Hrísey and Grímsey
☎ 462 7733
ℹ Bus terminal,
Hafnarstræti 82 ☎ 462
7733; www.eyjafjordur.is
🕐 Sep–May, Mon–Fri
8–5; Jun–Aug, Mon–Fri
7:30AM–7PM, Sat–Sun 8–7
↔ Grímsey (➤ 57), Mývatn
(➤ 19)

*High mountains form a
dramatic backdrop to the
town and its harbour*

Akureyri

**Despite its location so close to the Arctic Circle,
Iceland's northern capital has the reputation of a
banana belt. It may get more snow and cold
weather in winter than Reykjavík, but this is more
than compensated for by greater warmth and
sunshine in summer. Locals make the most of this
by growing trees and flowers everywhere – in tubs,
window boxes and gardens – and it's known as a
floral town. Artists also flourish here.**

Agriculturally, this is one of the richest areas in Iceland and
you'll see lots of red-roofed farms dotted along the shores
of Eyjafjörður. Farmers first settled here in Viking times,
when it became known as a trading area. However, the
town itself only developed in the late 18th century, in two
distinct halves – the old Danish town around Aðalstræti and
the Icelandic town around the modern harbour. They met
in the middle with the theatre in 1902, where you can still
see the old harbour walls. Akureyri now boasts a
population of 15,000 and its own university.

You can easily walk around the pleasant old centre in a
day. There are good shops and eating places, an interesting church, a lovely botanic gardens and numerous little
museums to explore. Einar Jónsson's famous statue 'The
Outlaw' stands on Eyrlandsvegur near the park (➤ 35). A
stroll past the old houses along Aðalstræti is a must. The
town claims the world's most northerly 18-hole golf
course, Jaðarsvöllur, and all are welcome at the Arctic
Open tournament, held through the hours of midnight sun
in June.

What to See in Akureyri

AKUREYRARKIRKJA ✪✪
In summer a steady stream of visitors makes its way up the long flight of steps from the corner of Hafnarstræti and Kaupvangsstræti to the white-painted church at the top. With its stumpy twin towers and square front it's not Iceland's most beautiful church but it's interesting nevertheless as a forerunner of Reykjavík's Hallgrímskirkja (➤ 16); also designed by Guðjón Samúelsson, it was built in 1940. Inside, the stained glass shows important scenes from Icelandic history. The distinguished central window in the chancel is a survivor of the old Coventry Cathedral in England. Removed for safekeeping during World War II it was eventually sold to an Icelander who presented it to the new church.

✛ 25D3
☎ 462 7700
🕐 Jun–Aug 10–12 and 2–4
♿ To avoid the steps, walk up Kaupvangsstræti and approach from the back
🎟 Free
❓ Service at 11AM, Sunday

KJARNASKÓGAR ✪✪
Carry on south of town towards the airport for a few kilometers and you'll reach this beautiful area of woodland, mainly birch and conifer, set on a sunny hillside. It's a favourite with local people at weekends – there are lots of walking trails and good places for picnics and barbecues.

✛ 25D3
✉ Just south of town on Route 821
🕐 Open access
♿ None
🎟 Free

MINJASAFN AKUREYRAR (FOLK MUSEUM) ✪✪✪
The town's beautifully presented museum occupies a modern building screened by trees on Aðalstræti. Displays, including a rare ship-burial on the the ground floor, bring the history of Iceland to life. The little church below it is part of the museum, moved to this location from Svalbarðseyri on the opposite shore.

✛ 25D3
✉ Aðalstræti 58
☎ 462 4162
🕐 Jun–Sep, daily 11–5; Sep–May, Sat 2–4
♿ None
🎟 Cheap
❓ Summer concerts held in the church

NONNAHÚS ✪
You can pick out 'Nonni's House' on Aðalstræti from the life-size statue in the garden of the pink house in front, of a friendly looking fellow in hat and cloak. Nonni was the nickname of Jesuit priest Jón Sveinsson (1857–1944), a widely travelled man who incorporated his own adventures into stories for children which in turn became famous across Europe.

✛ 25D3
✉ Aðalstræti 54a
☎ 462 3555
🕐 Jun–Aug, daily 10–5
♿ None
🎟 Cheap

The statue of Nonni, creator of the 'Nonni and Manni' stories for children

53

What to See in the North & Northeast

ASKJA ✪✪✪

If you want to get into the island's remote desert interior, then this is one of the places to head for. You can do it on a day's round trip from Reykjalíð but be warned – the track is demanding and 4WD essential. Route F88 passes through a desolate landscape of gritty black lava and unwholesome powdery yellow pumice, but it's worth the trip to see this vast caldera in the Dyngjufjöll mountains. It was formed as recently as 1875 when the nearby volcano of Víti erupted, smothering much of eastern Iceland in ash. In the southeast corner of this massive natural depression is a smaller caldera, holding the windswept expanse of Öskjuvatn, at 217m believed to be the deepest lake in the country.

Heading south on Route F88 towards Askja, you'll see a curiously symmetrical, black, flat-topped mountain looming ahead. This is Herðubreið, for centuries believed unclimbable because of its steep surrounding slopes of treacherous scree, until a German and an Icelander finally conquered it together in 1908. The greenery and vegetation here, fed by freshwater streams, come as something of a relief after all those barren miles of lava desert.

✚ 25E3

✉ On Route F88; access strictly limited to July and August, be prepared for extreme weather conditions

🍴 None

💷 Free

🔁 Tours from Mývatn pass through Herðubreið. Guided super-jeep tours
☎ 464 3940;
www.fjallasyn.is

The milky waters in the crater lake of Víti are warm enough for swimming

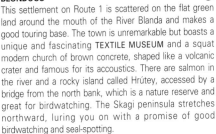

The modern church at Blönduós stands in splendid isolation on a hill above the town

BLÖNDUÓS ✪

This settlement on Route 1 is scattered on the flat green land around the mouth of the River Blanda and makes a good touring base. The town is unremarkable but boasts a unique and fascinating **TEXTILE MUSEUM** and a squat modern church of brown concrete, shaped like a volcanic crater and famous for its accoustics. There are salmon in the river and a rocky island called Hrútey, accessed by a bridge from the north bank, which is a nature reserve and great for birdwatching. The Skagi peninsula stretches northward, luring you on with a promise of good birdwatching and seal-spotting.

To the south of the town, don't miss the solitary stone-built church of Thingeyrar which marks a wealthy monastic site that was once central to the transcription of both the Bible and the Sagas; it has a fascinating interior with a star-painted ceiling and an unusual (English) altarpiece. Stand with your back to it and you'll find figures watching you from the gallery.

✚ 24C3
✉ 145km west of Akureyri
🍴 Various (£–££)
ℹ 452 4520 🕐 Jun–Aug 8AM–9PM

HEIMILISIÐNAÐARSAFNIÐ (TEXTILE MUSEUM)

✉ Árbraut 29, Blönduós
☎ 452 4067/452 4290; www.simnet.is/textile
🕐 Jun–Aug, daily 10–5
👜 Cheap

BORGAFJÖRÐUR EYSTRI ✪ (BAKKAGERÐI)

For a town with two names, this is not a big one but is beautifully set on a broad bay, with a green valley behind and the dramatic mountain of Dyrfjöll (1136m) beyond. With such a fine location, it's no surprise to know that the elves live around here in goodly numbers, notably inhabiting the small mound-with-a-view, Álfaborg. Look out for semi-precious stones at your feet – you can see examples in the **ÁLFASTEINN** museum and shop. Iceland's famous landscape painter Jóhannes S Kjarval was raised near by at Geitavík, and you'll recognise the backdrop in his altarpiece in the church with Christ standing on Álfaborg.

✚ 25F3
✉ 336km east of Akureyri, on Route 94

ÁLFASTEINN

☎ 472 9977; www.alfasteinn.is
🕐 Jun–Aug, daily 10–6; Sep–May, Mon–Fri 10–12 and 1–5
👜 Free

25D4

On Route 82, 44km north of Akureyri

Brekka Restaurant on Hrísey serves excellent Galloway beef, as well as lighter snacks ☎ 466 1751

Scheduled ferry to Hrísey and Grímsey

Whale-watching tours ☎ 466 3355

HVOLL (FOLK MUSEUM)

Karlsrauðatorg

☎ 466 1497

Jun–Aug daily 11–6 and on request

Cheap

DALVÍK

Looking at this busy fishing town today there's nothing to show that it was almost destroyed by a massive earthquake in 1934. It's beautifully set near the mouth of Eyjafjörður, with mountains behind and a view of the large island of Hrísey across the water. It's worth the short ferry ride to enjoy the peace and quiet of the nature reserve here. Hrísey's other claim to fame is as a quarantine island for livestock and pets coming into Iceland.

The FOLK MUSEUM in Dalvík has displays dedicated to local giant Jóhann Pétursson, who grew to 2.34m high and became a Hollywood film star. Behind the town you can explore the interesting wetlands of Svarfaðardalur; a good leaflet, available locally, lists the marsh plants here and details of several walks. To the north, the precipitous road leads on to Ólafsfjörður; the silver ship memorial overlooking the fjord is to a local boat-builder, Eyvindur Jónsson, who died in 1746.

25D3

Off Route 1

Coffee and snacks (£–££) at Fosshóll, also some accommodation ☎ 464 3108

All the tour buses stop here

None

Free

Mývatn (➤ 19); Akureyri (➤ 52)

GOÐAFOSS

Travelling along the road from Akureyri to Mývatn you'll see what looks like a cloud of smoke over to your right, as though someone were burning off the heather. This is spray from the mighty horseshoe falls of Goðafoss; you can park at the petrol station-cum-store at Fosshóll, cross the deep gorge of the river Skjálfandafljót and follow the well-worn path to view this beautiful waterfall. They're called the 'falls of the gods' after an incident in AD 1000, when the Lawspeaker at the Althing decided in favour of the country becoming Christian and duly threw all his pagan idols in the water on his way home. This is a good place to hunt for wild flowers in the heath – look out for the delicate white flowers of mountain avens.

The inter-island ferry waits in Dalvík harbour

GRÍMSEY ✪

Contrary to popular expectation, most of Iceland lies south of the Arctic Circle, but this windswept island some 40km off shore is the exception, straddling the line at its northern tip. On a still pink summer's evening when the sun never quite sets on the horizon and the Arctic terns swoop overhead it can seem a romantic spot, but the rest of the time there's not much to recommend it. The obligatory fingerpost which marks the circle line is a 25-minute walk up from the harbour, and offers the best photo-opportunity. To the north the razorbills, puffins and kittiwakes that once formed an important part of the island's economy nest noisily on the cliffs.

➕ 25D4
✉ 41km north of mainland
🍴 Meals and limited accommodation at Guesthouse Básar
☎ 467 3103 (£££)
🚢 Regular ferry from Dalvík, and excursion boat. Scheduled flights from Akureyri with Air Iceland
☎ 460 7000
🔁 Dalvík (► 56); Akureyri (► 52)

HÓLAR ✪✪

Waymarked footpaths lead you around this attractive corner of the Haltadalur valley. The first ever translation of the Bible in Icelandic was printed at Hólar in 1584. Until

1798 it was the seat of the northern bishopric, and the present cathedral is the fifth to be built here. It's worth a look in for the unusual chunky font of Greenland stone and the wonderfully vivid three-dimensional altarpiece, presented by Jón Arason, last Catholic bishop of Iceland, who served here from 1524–50. After his execution at Skálholt (► 46) his body was brought here and buried under the separate, tall belltower. Hólar is now home to a school and an agricultural college, open in summer.

➕ 24C4
✉ On Route 767, 100km east of Blönduós
🕐 Church open daily
🍴 Summer snack bar in school building.
ℹ 455 6333/455 6300
♿ None
🎟 Free
❓ Guided tours of the church available 9–5; www.holar.is

Above: *the foaming waters of Goðafoss*
Left: *climb the tall tower at Hólar for spectacular views over the valley*

🚩 25D4

✉ On Route 85, 91km northeast of Akureyri

🍴 Restaurant/café (££)

🚢 Whale-watching tours from traditional wooden fishing boats, may be combined with puffin-watching on Lundey island

♿ None

❓ For an introduction to the high-tech world of fish processing, central to Iceland's economy, the Whale Centre can arrange for a guided tour of the local freezing plant – don't miss it!

HVALAMIÐSTÖÐIN (WHALE CENTRE)

✉ Hafnarstétt

☎ 464 2520

🕐 Flexible opening daily, May to mid-Sep 10–5, Jun–Aug 9–9

💶 Cheap

Right: *Húsavík is dominated by its spendid Norwegian church*
Below: *the barren lands of the interior near Hveravellir*

HÚSAVÍK ✪✪✪

Whale-watching has become one of Iceland's most popular tourist activities and Húsavík, a pleasant fishing town on the western shore of the rolling Tjörnes peninsula, is deservedly its capital. Spotting success rates are higher here than anywhere else – you're more or less guaranteed a sighting of the small minke whales, and there's a good chance you'll see the nobbly snouts and classic tail-flukes of humpback whales here too. If the conditions are right, you may even be lucky enough to spot fin, sei and killer whales (orcas). Take binoculars and sun-glasses with you – the glare from the surface of the sea as you scour it for telltale puffs of whale-spout can be tiring. Don't miss a visit to the WHALE CENTRE for a better under-standing of these great sea-creatures – there are whole skeletons to wonder at, a touch table (try the shark skin!) and lots of fascinating information about the whales and dolphins found around Iceland.

JÖKULSÁRGLJÚFUR (➤ 17, TOP TEN)

KJÖLUR ✪✪

The high road through the interior known as Kjalvegur follows an old route between north and south which has been used since earliest times. Kjölur is the bare valley at the mid-point sandwiched between the Langjökull and Hofsjökull glaciers. To the north, the road passes through high boggy country towards Blöndudalur; to the south the landscape is black and volcanic, stained with minerals and steaming areas of mud and sulphur. It feels cold here – there's a summer ski centre to the southeast on the flanks of Kerlingarfjöll. However, Kjölur holds a surprise – the geothermal oasis of Hveravellir, with hot springs of clear water, alpine flowers, a touring hut and campsite – and a weather station that is cut off from the world for most of the year. You can drive this route in a day in summer if the conditions are good ; in winter it's for the off-roaders.

🗺 24C2
✉ Route F35 runs between Gullfoss and Blöndudalur
🍴 None
🚌 Scheduled summer buses take this route between Reykjavik and Akureyri
↔ Gullfoss (➤ 14–15)

MÝVATN (➤ 19, TOP TEN)

SAURBÆR ✪✪✪

The lovely sunny valley to the south of Akureyri is worth exploring for its four quite different churches, each found on a farm. You can loop up the west side of the valley on the 821 to Saurbær and return on the opposite side (about 55km). At Grund there is a large exotic-looking affair, with a red-painted onion dome and turrets, dating from 1905. The church at Saurbær is a more cosy traditional structure of timber and turf with a bell over the front door. It's from 1858 and marks the spot of a much older convent. On the return trip, the pretty white church at Möðruvellir has a strange wooden cage in the churchyard, a bell gate from 1781. The fourth church of interest is Munkathverá, on a former monastic site and more typical of the old Lutheran churches. The memorial beside it is to Jón Arason, last Catholic bishop of Iceland, who was born near by.

🗺 25D3
✉ Saurbær is 27km south of Akureyri
🎟 Free
↔ Akureyri (➤ 52)
❓ Ask locally for keys if locked; the farm dogs can be noisy and nosy, but not generally dangerous

The turf church at Saurbær is one of only six left in Iceland

From Husavík to Mývatn

Distance
195km

Time
All day, with pauses for exploration

Start/end point
Húsavík
✚ 25D4

Lunch
Hótel Gígur (££–£££)
✉ near Reykjalíð
☎ 464 4455

Fossil Museum
✉ Hallbjarnastaðir
☎ 464 1968
🕐 Jun–Aug 10–6

The monument to Einar Benediktson, who died in 1940; his father was a politician prominent in the struggle for Icelandic independence

Start from Húsavík and take Route 85 north up the coast.

Enjoy the views west to the cake-shaped island of Lundey, teeming with puffins through summer, and even of Grímsey on a clear day. After 4km, the roadside monument is to poet Einar Benediktson.

Continue for 9km and turn into Hallbjarnastaðir to see the fossil museum. Retrace your route and after 3km turn right to Tjörneshöfn. The road down to the harbour is steep and muddy – walk down if in doubt.

This is the best place to see the lines of compressed fossil shells in the cliffs.

Return to Húsavík, and stay on Route 85 towards Akureyri, crossing a big lava field covered with birch trees. After 39km turn left onto Route 845 for Laxárvirkjun.

This soon brings you to the pretty gabled farmhouse museum of Grenjaðarstaður; there's an ancient runic gravestone in the churchyard.

Return to Route 85 and turn left, to Laugar. At the junction with Route 1 turn left for Mývatn. Keep on Route 1 around the southern shore of the lake.

Lunch at the Hótel Gígur and stroll through green mounds scattered with periwinkles, or go on to Höfði for a picnic and walk through the birchwoods. Look out for whooper swans, tufted ducks, widgeon and Barrow's goldeneye on the lake, and listen for the drumming of snipe.

Continue to Reykjahlíð, and keep right on Route 1 for the sulphurous geothermal area of Námafjall, and Krafla power station 7km further on. Return to Reykjahlíð and bear right on Route 86 to return across the high moors to Húsavík.

SIGLUFJÖRÐUR ✪✪✪

This quiet little town on the northern coast, hemmed in by steep mountains and for years accessible only by sea, played a key role in the rapid growth of the Icelandic economy in the last century. For this was a herring boom town, alive with thousands of migratory workers throughout the season, its sheltered fjord packed with fishing boats. In 1916 alone 200,000 barrels of salted herring were exported from here, and at the height of the boom in the 1940s the town held 23 salting stations and 5 processing factories. Overfishing led to a crash of herring stocks in the 1960s and Siglufjörður's heyday came to an end. It's a story well-told in photographs, film and memorabilia at the **MUSEUM** in the old herring station of Roaldsbrakki. On summer weekends it's brought to life again with the 'herring show' – a funny, lively dramatisation of fishery days. Although it's in Icelandic you'll understand what's going on and can join in the dancing at the end.

✚ 24C4
✉ Route 76, 192km northwest of Akureyri
ℹ 460 5600/467 1604

SÍLDARMINJASAFNIÐ (HERRING ERA MUSEUM)
☎ 467 1604
✉ Snorragata
🕐 Jun-Aug, daily 10-6; spring and autumn 1–5
💷 Cheap   ♿ None
❓ Herring show Jul–Aug, weekends 3PM

Re-enacting the herring boom at Siglufjörður's, museum

VOPNAFJÖRÐUR ✪

It's rumoured that Father Christmas lives to the south of this remote East Fjords town in the hill known as Smjörfjöll ('butter mountain') – he probably comes here for the excellent fishing on the Selá and other local rivers. You'll climb the breathtaking hairpin bends on this mountain if you're travelling on the 917, and the views from the top are worth it. The settlement itself was once an important trading post but now concentrates on fisheries, with a harbour conveniently sheltered by low green islands. Route 85 brings you over some dreary high moors, but around the mountain of Bustarfell the views get more interesting and there's a charming old turf-clad farm museum there.

✚ 25F4
✉ 233km east of Akureyri
ℹ Hafnarbyggð 7   ☎ 473 1565

BYGGÐASAFN (FOLK MUSEUM)
✉ Bustarfell
☎ 473 1466
🕐 Jun–Sep, daily 10–6
♿ None
💷 Cheap

Food & Drink

Of necessity Icelanders live around the coastline of their island and, since fishing supports some 70 per cent of the economy, it's not really surprising that fish features largely in their diet.

Haddock (*ýsa*) is the national favourite, fresh and boiled or fried lightly. Cod (*thorskur*) is largely exported but you may find delicacies such as cod chins on the menu – try them, they are rich and delicious. Catfish (*steinbítur*) and halibut (*lúða*) are also widely available, and pickled herring (*síld*) is often served at breakfast. You'll see fish drying on wooden racks along the coast; this used to be a staple food to see poor farmers through the winter but now it's something of a delicacy – called *harðfiskur*, it looks like shredded loofah and has a mild, not unpleasant fish taste, eaten smeared with butter (*smjör*). Try it at the market in Kolaportið (➤ 80) before you buy. Pickling fish in whey is a speciality, celebrated in the Thorrablót festival in February.

Shellfish are also excellent, notably the small lobster (*humar*). For freshwater fish, try the salmon (*lax*), trout (*silungur*) and Arctic char (*bleikja*).

The most notorious Icelandic dish is carefully rotted shark flesh (*hákarl*) which, when swilled down with a shot of the spirit *brennivín*, is supposed to induce a rapid state of intoxication – try it if you dare.

Icelanders boast that their lamb, fed on good pasture, comes ready-seasoned and it's certainly very good. Roasted, it's a traditional Sunday lunch, but you'll also find it salted (*saltkjöt*) and, particularly around Christmas, smoked like ham (*hangikjöt*). Singed sheep head is a less

Icelandic seafood is some of the freshest and best in the world

appealing traditional item, eaten hot or cold, and you can buy it ready-pressed and gelled (sviðasulta).

If you are determined to try the unusual, some restaurants serve puffin, guillemot and even fulmar, and at certain times you'll also see their mottled eggs for sale. The Icelanders have been eating them for years without denting the population, so don't feel too bad about it.

A ready supply of fruit and vegetables came late to this remote island, but the wonders of geothermal power harnessed to green-houses in centres such as Hveragerði (➤ 42) mean that much more is now available, if not cheap. Bananas are actually grown in Akureyri.

Small cinnamon biscuits (kex) can be bought by the bagfull in any supermarket – and look out for the tasty donut knot, kleinur. A sweet, dark rye-bread is cooked slowly in the hot lava (rúgbrauð), and at Christmas fragile flat cakes of thinly rolled and cut pastry are deep-fried (laufabrauð – see them out of season in the Christmas shop at Akureyri). Rye pancakes (flatbrauð) and large sweet pancakes are also eaten.

The low-fat dairy product skyr is widely available. Somewhere between cream cheese and yogurt, it is good served with cream and sugar or fresh fruit, and it also makes an excellent basis for cheesecake. Milk labelling can be confusing — nýmjólk is the normal stuff, while léttmjólk is semi-skimmed, undanrenna is skimmed and súrmjólk like thin yogurt. And of course ice-cream (ís) is eaten everywhere.

Lamb from the wiry sheep who roam the hills in summer and winter indoors is suprisingly tender

63

The South & Southeast

This part of Iceland is dominated by the great ice-cap of Vatnajökull, which has shaped everything around it. Tongues of glacier ooze down between the mountains, and floodwaters have produced the vast desolate gravel and sand expanses (*sandur*) of Mýrdalssandur and Skeiðarársandur. The coastal lagoons around Höfn teem with migratory birds in spring and autumn, and after the steep fjords of the eastern coastline, the more expansive landscape of Fljótsdalur is welcome relief.

> *'I will not pretend that the landscape of Iceland is always beautiful. It is only so when the sky is clear. And on grey days it is sad, but never sullen.'*

GEORGE SEAVER,
Icelandic Yesterdays (1935)

———————●———————

Reyðarfjöður lies on the East Fjords

What to See in the South & Southeast

BREIÐDALSVÍK ✪

An unexceptional village of low modern houses (winter gales in 2000 blew one of the last wooden houses to smithereens), Breiðdalsvík is nevertheless magnificent in its surroundings, with colourful rhyolite mountains tipped up to 1,200m high behind, and lots of little bays popular with seals and eider ducks in front. The gradually retreating sea has left big gravel beds in the middle of the wide valley and so it's not surprising that early settlers, making their first landfalls here, chose to stay up the road at Snæhvammur– burial artefacts 1,000 years old were discovered here (now in the National Museum, Reykjavík). In 1942 a German aircraft attacked the village along with the spectacular lighthouse at Kambanes.

DJÚPIVOGUR ✪✪✪

The houses of Djúpivogur perch prettily among the rocks around the harbour on this rugged peninsula, with fabulous views out to the skerries around the low island of Papey. It seems incredible today that the village should have been a target for North African pirates in 1627. Roman coins were discovered to the west, prompting speculation that the Romans also made it here, but it's now thought more likely that they were part of some Viking's plunder from Britain. The old **LANGABÚÐ** warehouse has an extraordinary museum of heads carved by local sculptor Ríkarður Jónsson (1888–1977), and a coffee shop. The area is famous for its zeolites – round stones which crack open to reveal beautiful crystals. Take a half-day boat trip to Papey,

🕂 25F3
✉ 82km southeast of Egilsstaðir
🍽 Hótel Bláfell, Sólvellir 14
☎ 475 6770
📷 Wildlife boat tours of islands in the area to see birds, seals and whales
☎ 864 0246/475 6646

Below: *racks for drying fish – a familiar sight above the shore near Breiðdalsvík*

🕂 25F2
✉ 146km south of Egilsstaðir
📷 Cruises to Papey May–Sep ☎ 478 8183/478 8119

LANGABÚÐ
☎ 478 8220
🕐 Jun–Aug, daily 10–6
🍽 Pleasant summer café at Langabúð
♿ None
💰 Cheap

deserted now, but still with a tiny wooden church and lots of sea birds – the name suggests that its first settlers were Irish monks, probably scared off by Norse newcomers. The steep mountain ridge behind the town is Búlandstindur.

The black sands of Dyrhólaós on the route to Dyrhólaey

DYRHÓLAEY ✪✪✪

This sheer headland jutting out some 120m above the sea is a wildlife sanctuary and the southernmost point of mainland Iceland. It is reached via a causeway through hoodoos and a steep track up to the lighthouse. At its narrowest point the rock forms a natural arch over the water, big enough for tourist craft to sail through comfortably. A black sandy beach and another headland with picturesque pointed rock stacks at the end separate Dyrhólaey from the village of Vík, which has the unfortunate claim to be wetter than anywhere else in the country; more happily, it's the access point for the magnificent Mýrdalsjökull glacier.

✚ 24C1

✉ On route 218, 5km off of Route 1

🅖 Open access, except at height of sea bird breeding season

🚍 Boat tours around Dyrhólaey ☎ 487 8500

🛈 Brydebúd, Víkurbraut 28, Vík ☎ 487 1395

EGILSSTAÐIR ✪✪

Egilsstaðir lies about as far away from Reykjavík as you can get without leaving the ring road. It's a growing holiday town, lively with its own importance. The town's attractions include an open-air market and the local history museum for East Iceland, but its chief interest for visitors (apart from its excellent sunshine record) is its setting on the river Lagarfljót. This flows down from the glacier of Vatnajökull, broadening to the south of town into the long, milky-blue lake of Lögurinn, which comes complete with its own shape-changing monster, the Lagarfljótsormurinn, and a forest at Hallormsstaður (► 68). There's lots to do here if you're feeling active including reindeer hunting, as well as the more usual hiking, cycling, horse riding, skiing and trout fishing.

✚ 25F3

✉ Route 1, 698km east of Reykjavík

🚌 Scheduled coach service daily from Reykjavík and Akureyri

🍴 Range of cafés

🛈 Kaupvangur 6 ☎ 471 2320; www.egilsstadir.is

❓ Summer cruises on the lake to Atlavík, Tue–Sun. ☎ 471 2900. Also trips to Snæfell (► 72)

HALLORMSSTAÐUR ⊙

It is believed that Iceland was once covered in trees, and reafforestation to prevent soil erosion is a major concern today. This is the largest forestry plantation in the country, covering some 740sq km, and it provides a pleasant recreation area with walking trails and horse riding as well as a lovely campsite on the sandy lake shore at Atlavík. The tallest tree on the site is a Russian larch, planted in 1938 in memory of a forester.

🕇 25F3
✉ On eastern shore of lake Lögurinn, on route 931
☎ 471 1774 (Atlavík campsite)
🍴 Snacks at Fosshótel Hallormsstaður (£–££)
✋ Open access
❓ Easy access from Egilsstaðir

🕇 25E2
✉ On route 1, 459km east of Reykjavík
🍴 Range of cafés and restaurants (£–£££)
ℹ Hafnarbraut 52 ☎ 478 1500
↔ Vatnajökull (► 72); Jökulsárlón (► 18)
❓ Hátíð á Höfn (Lobster Festival) in early July with music, dance, competitions and feasting

Above: *looking east up the coastline towards Höfn*

HÖFN ⊙⊙⊙

Try saying 'hup'n' while breathing in sharply, and you'll be somewhere near the correct pronunciation of this harbour town. Protected from the sea by two narrow spits of land, the town is beautifully set between two lagoons in a green oasis at the foot of sweeping mountains. For years it could only be reached by road from the north, but completion of the ring road in 1974 ended its isolation. Today Höfn's a convenient centre for exploring Vatnajökull and Jökulsárlón. The town has a new Glacier Exhibition Centre on Hafnarbraut. It's well worth exploring the magnificent moss-covered valleys to the east, and the Lónsvík shore, teeming with eiders, swans and wild geese.

JÖKULSÁRLÓN (► 18, TOP TEN)

🕇 25D1
✉ Route 1, 258km east of Reykjavík
🍴 Snacks at service station (£)
ℹ Klausturvellir 10 ☎ 487 4840/487 4620

KIRKJUBÆJARKLAUSTUR ⊙⊙

According to *Landnámabók* this area was first settled by Irish monks. Benedictine nuns occupied the site until 1550, and they are remembered in local place-names, such as the large outcrop of rock to the southwest called Systrastapi (Sisters' Rock). A natural feature called Kirkjugólf can be seen just off the junction with Route 203 – the smoothed tops of perfectly interlocking basalt rock columns, it looks like the tiled floor of a church (or a municipal pavement). The settlement lies in the shadow of

the petrified lava-flow from the appallingly destructive volcano Laki; in 1783 the local hellfire preacher Jón Steingrímsson halted the lava just outside the village with his prayers. Summer tours from here can take you up the F206 to see the spectacular Lakakígar crater row.

Above: *multicoloured scoria and petrified lava at Landmannalaugar*
Inset: *basalt columns form a natural pavement at Kirkjubæjarklaustur*

LANDMANNALAUGAR ✪✪✪

Described as one of Iceland's 'natural jewels', this is certainly one of the most extensive and beautiful geothermal landscapes you'll see, surrounded by multicoloured rhyolite mountains. Brennisteinsalda is just one of the highlights, streaked red, blue-grey and yellow, with all the colours in between and green moss for good measure. The combination of natural hot steam and cold fresh spring water makes the bathing pools just the right temperature. Don't hurry your visit, allowing at least a couple of days to explore the area – it's a long way from anywhere else and there's so much to discover – but note that accommodation is limited, and it gets very busy in summer.

🚻 24C2
✉ On Route F208, 100km north of Route 1
🍴 Nearest coffee stop and petrol is Hrauneyjafosstöð, at junction of F208 and F26
🔄 Four-day trek to Thórsmörk (➤ 47) is a classic long distance path
❓ 4WD essential, and note the roads may be closed at short notice even in summer because of flooding

REYÐARFJÖRÐUR ✪✪

The large number of recycled Nissen huts around Reyðarfjörður rather give the game away – there was an Allied base here during World War II, and you can discover more about this period at the MUSEUM in the town. It's normally a quiet fishing town, on the sunny side of the biggest of the East Fjords, with a pleasing mix of old and new houses. It's on the road to Eskifjörður, and reached via a sweeping mountain pass from Egilsstaðir.

🚻 25F3
✉ On Route 92, 34km south of Egilsstaðir

STRÍÐSÁRASAFNIÐ (WORLD WAR II MUSEUM)
✉ Spítalakamp, V/Hæðagerði
☎ 470 9095
🕐 Jun–Aug, daily 1–6

+ 25F3
✉ 292km east of Akureyri, on Route 93
🍴 Snacks at pleasant Hótel Seyðisfjördur, Austurvegur 3 ☎ 472 1460
🚢 Weekly ferry *Norræna* sails to Faroes, Shetland, Norway and Denmark; May–Sep, Thu ☎ 472 1111
ℹ *Austfar*, Fjarðargata 8 ☎ 472 1111
❓ Arts and crafts market on summer Wed PM and Thu AM to coincide with ferry

SEYÐISFJÖRÐUR ✪✪

Old wooden Norwegian-style houses and a pretty blue-painted church make this one of the loveliest coastal towns in Iceland. It's set at the head of a narrow fjord, surrounded by steep mountains, and it declined into its current genteel state after the herring boom. Artist Nina Tryggvadóttir was born in one of the merchants' houses on the central 'Ridge' in 1913. The church is particularly attractive inside and so well worth a look – if locked, knock at a neighbouring house for the key. The town has been the victim of avalanches and landslips over the years, and the twisted girder 'sculpture' at the town's northern entrance is evidence of the destruction caused by the last. You may spot rare harlequin ducks on the river behind the town.

SKAFTAFELL (➤ 20, TOP TEN)

+ 24C1
✉ 154km east of Reykjavik
☎ 487 8845
⏰ Open daily, Jun–Aug 9–6:30; Sep–May 10–5
🍴 Edda hotel in Skógar (summer only)
♿ Few
 Cheap

Above: *a picture-book scene at Seyðisfjöður*

SKÓGAR ✪✪✪

Don't miss this folk museum, tucked under the hills north of the ring road, near the southern point of the country. It's an outstanding and entertaining collection, started by curator Thórður Tómason when he was 14, with everything from Viking buttons to Iceland's first radio set (imported from Germany). Notably there's a fully rigged fishing boat which is the centrepiece of a fascinating fisheries and whaling exhibition, as well as historic costumes, embroidery, carved bedboards and all sorts of other domestic items, including rams' condoms, moulds for horn spoons and a lethally weighted mousetrap. Outside you can explore old turf-clad farmhouses, a school and a beautiful wooden church. If you're lucky, the curator himself will be on hand to show you around and play the harmoniums for you – be prepared to sing along. The 60m waterfall at Skógar is also well worth a look.

Skaftafell

Two walks lead from the visitor centre: a short one to the glacier, and this longer one to the waterfall of Svartifoss.

Walk towards campsite, and bear right along gravel path. Take signed path to Svartifoss up hill, zigzagging through low birch and willow. Keep on the main path, cross a wooden bridge and climb the side of the gorge to reach the high Hundarfoss waterfall. Where the path branches keep right up the slope.

There are good views behind you over the plain, with rivers braiding across the gravel towards the sea. You can also see the broad snout of Skeiðarárjökull to the east.

Pass the smaller waterfall, Magnúsarfoss, and keep right, following signs for Svartifoss. Continue across open area of moss, heather and crowberries.

Svartifoss, down to your left, appears as a dramatic black gash in the hillside. Columnar basalt forms an echoing natural amphitheatre of hanging columns, like organ pipes, surrounding the central water plume. The pointed mountain ahead is Skarðatindur, 1385m.

Follow the precipitous path which can be slippery down to falls.

Enjoy a drink of the clear water and picnic on the rocks.

Cross the bridge and climb the rocky path – red-paint markers show the way. Turn right at finger post, up the steep hill to Sjónasker.

It's worth the long haul up for views of the mountains from the viewing table.

Head back down hill, past finger post, following signs to Tjaldsvæði (campsite). Cross the stream and keep left at fork. At the two bridges, turn left and cross the stream above Hundarfoss. Retrace your steps down the main path back to visitor centre.

Distance
4km

Time
Allow two hours, longer with a picnic stop

Start/end point
A circular walk, start from the National Park Visitor Centre
✚ 25D2

Lunch
Take a picnic to eat at the falls

An arc of basalt columns makes Svartifoss instantly recognisable among Icelandic waterfalls

🕀 25E3
✉ Access via F910 from
Fljótsdalur

*A snow tractor hauls
visitors onto Vatnajökull
for fantastic views over
Iceland's southern coast*

SNÆFELL ✪

This old, snow-capped volcano, 1,833m high, lies to the northeast of Vatnajökull, in an area of the interior most accessible from Fljótsdalur, and even then only in summer and with 4WD. One of the principal reasons to visit, apart from the fabulous views, is the chance of seeing wild reindeer. They graze on the tundra-like moss, lichen and grass on the moors up here, and more alarmingly, the shoots of young trees. They were first introduced from Norway at the end of the 18th century to provide an extra source of food for people. Winters proved too harsh and the experiment was never very successful, but this stock have survived and there are now several thousand roaming the hillsides. In a cold spring or autumn, you may find them nearer the coast.

🕀 25D2
❓ Join a tour from Höfn
(► 68) up to
Skálafellsjökull for the
best access on to the
glacier – tours include
guided snow scooter or
snow tractor rides, and
are expensive but well
worth it for the views and
experience

VATNAJÖKULL ✪✪✪

Vatnajökull actually dates from a mini-Ice Age only 2,500 years ago. The biggest ice-cap in Europe (in fact, at over 8000sq km, bigger than all the others put together), it is a temperate glacier, inherently unstable, which makes life difficult and sometimes dangerous for those who live around its edges. (Not that this stops visitors having a fine time exploring on skidoos.) For it lies like a smothering 1km-thick, cold but not entirely frozen, blanket over the top of several live volcanoes, and when they errupt – as Grímsvötn did in 1996 – the ice quickly melts. The meltwater gathers in under-ice lakes until it overflows in a massive *hlaup*, bringing quantities of mud, rock and icebergs sweeping down onto the plains, reshaping the landscape as it goes. Its glacier fingers spread along the southern coast of Iceland, most beautifully at Jökulsárlón (► 18).

Where To...

Above: *maritime exhibition at the Folk Museum, Skógar*
Right: *a folksy house-sign covered in miniatures*

Reykjavík

Prices

Approximate prices for a two-course meal without wine

£   = under 1,000ISK
££ = 1,000–2,000ISK
£££ = over 2,000ISK

Home brew

Egils is probably the best known brand of Icelandic beer, named after a Viking Saga hero and consumed everywhere since the ban on beer was lifted in 1989. Egils also manufacture soft drinks and among the more unusual of these is Egils Malt Extrakt. When poured into the glass with a corresponding can of fizzy orangeade, the drink becomes a Christmas favourite.

A NAESTU GROSUM (£)

Readers highly recommend this downtown vegetarian restaurant, with buffet-style section, home-made bread and cakes and organic wines.

📧 Laugavegur 20b ☎ 552 8410 🕐 Mon–Sat lunch and dinner, Sun dinner only

CAFÉ PARIS (£)

The green building on the corner of Austervöllur square – get yourself a window table and watch the world go by. Can be very busy. Pancakes with ice-cream are especially good.

📧 Austervöllur ☎ 551 1020 🕐 Lunch and dinner

DELI (£)

For food on the run, don't miss this little snack bar at the bottom of Skolavörðustígur. Look through to the kitchen to see your food being freshly prepared with top quality ingredients – pasta salads, panini with sundried tomatoes and mozzarella, focaccia, pizza and tasty sandwiches. All this, and internet access too!

📧 Bankastræti 14 ☎ 551 6000 🕐 10–7

EINAR BEN (££–£££)

Set in the upper part of an elegant old red townhouse, above a woollen goods shop, this stylish restaurant and bar is close to the new tourist information centre. Try langousitine tails with salt cod cannelloni, or flounder fillets in a parsley crust, followed by white chocolate cheesecake with wild strawberry ice cream.

📧 Ingólfstorg ☎ 511 5090 🕐 Dinner

ELDSMIÐJAN (£)

Wonderful smells waft from the wood-fired oven as you enter this corner-set pizza house, just down from the Hallgrímskirkja. It's good, simple food at its best. Downstairs is a busy takeaway and upstairs it's cosy, with room for just a few to sit. The menus come in all the varieties you'd expect, but with some interesting variations. Try a fiery Hekla; and an *ostagerðarmannsins* (old cheesemaker) comes with mozarella, cream cheese, parmesan and blue cheese.

📧 Bragagötu 38A ☎ 562 3838 🕐 Lunch and dinner

FYLGIFISKAR (£–££)

Enjoy soup and a choice of three hot dishes at this remarkable seafish emporium, overlooking Laugardalur. Owner Guðbörg Glóð Logadottír has studied all aspects of fish preparation, and serves over 30 different kinds, all fresh and flavoursome, delicately spiced. You can also buy it ready prepared to cook yourself. Sesam Bleikja – Arctic char with sesame, corriander and chilli – is a speciality.

📧 Suðurlandsbraut 10 ☎ 533 1303 🕐 Lunch Mon–Fri, and Sat in winter

GALLERY RESTAURANT (£££)

This is the restaurant of the famous Hótel Holt and worth a visit even if you're not staying there. Fine cuisine served in plush surroundings that feel like a private art gallery. Seafood, of course, dominates the menu, and the wine list is extensive.

✉ Bergstaðastræti 37 ☎ 552 5700 🕐 Lunch and dinner

GRÆNN KOSTUR (£)

Tasty vegetarian meals served fast-food style, and including the best houmous in town. Emphasis on health food, avoiding yeast, sugar, wheat, eggs and milk products.

✉ Skólavörðustígur 8b ☎ 552 2028 🕐 Lunch and dinner

KAFFI SÓLON (£)

Wooden chairs, candles and art on the walls give this corner restaurant a cosmopolitan air, and it's perfectly set for a lunchtime break when you've been shopping 'til you're dropping on Laugavegur. Sample the bread and tapenade, or perhaps the seafood soup, and leave room for the cake of the day. Good range of vegetarian choices, too.

✉ Bankastræti 7A ☎ 562 3232 🕐 Lunch and dinner

KÍNA-HÚSIÐ (£–£££)

If you fancy a change, try this top Chinese restaurant in the town centre. You can't miss it – it's painted bright red for luck. Sample lobster in a curry sauce, fish with bamboo shoots and mushrooms, or perhaps sweet and sour duck. Special cheaper lunchtime menus.

✉ Lækjargata 8 ☎ 551 1014 🕐 Lunch and dinner, closed Sat and Sun lunch

LÆKJARBREKKA (££–£££)

The old wooden house by the tourist information office is one of Reykjavík's most popular restaurants, famous for its traditional dishes including mountain lamb and a summer lobster feast. The atmosphere is cosy behind the lace curtains, and the food delicious.

✉ Bankastræti 2 ☎ 551 4430 🕐 Lunch and dinner

PERLAN (£££)

Gives a whole new meaning to the term 'top restaurant', built in a revolving glass dome on the city's hot water tanks. Dining is formal but excellent – this is where locals come for an expensive treat.

✉ Öskjuhlið ☎ 562 0200 🕐 Lunch and dinner

RESTAURANT HORNIÐ (£–££)

An old golden-painted restaurant and bar high on a corner near the post office, serving a wide range of fresh seafood, pizza and pasta. The food is terrific and affordable – try the mixed seafood platter or the salmon steaks.

✉ Hafnarstræti 15 ☎ 551 3340 Lunch and dinner

SKÓLABRÚ (£–£££)

This is up-market food at its most elaborate, in a pleasing old white house just off Austurvöller square. You could try a starter of smoked puffin, gannet and guillemot, followed perhaps by breast of duck with glazed red onions and red cabbage with corriander and ginger peas. Fixed menus and à la carte.

✉ Pósthússtræti 17 ☎ 562 4455 🕐 Lunch and dinner

SVARTA KAFFIÐ (£–££)

Upstairs bar and coffee house on Laugavegur with an unusual but very tasty lunchtime speciality – súpa í brauði, which is home-made soup served in a crusty bread roll. Light meals.

✉ Laugavegur 54 ☎ 551 2999 🕐 Lunch and dinner

THRÍR FRAKKAR (££–£££)

A curious restaurant with a popular reputation for fish, and an owner with a distinctive sense of humour – the name can mean three Frenchmen or three

Beer and wine

Drinking in Iceland is an expensive business, so be prepared. A pint of Guinness in Reykjavík will knock you back about £5 (600ISK) and lager is a similar price, rising to £8 (1,000ISK). A bottle of wine with your meal could cost you as much as six times the supermarket price at home, so you may prefer to buy by the glass. Alcohol for private consumption is sold only through a limited number of government outlets. Purchasing this way, it is about twice the UK price for wine, beer and spirits, though a similar level for champagne!

Tipping

There is no tradition of tipping in Iceland, and giving a tip may cause offence.

Attitudes to alcohol
Icelanders tend to save it all for Friday and Saturday night, then drink to get drunk – and there's not much middle ground. The problems of alcohol abuse are recognised, and tackled in several ways. For a start, you must be over the age of 20 to purchase a drink. Advertising of alcohol is also banned and you can only buy it from government outlet stores, which are not always easy to spot – there's one discreetly in the middle of Reykjavík, on Austurstræti.

overcoats, and he chose the latter. Décor has an off-beat kitsch feel – note the dried fish clock on the wall. You can taste a traditional Icelandic dish of combined fish and potato (*plokkfiskur*), served with black bread. Other fish dishes tend to be served with strong, creamy sauces. Soup of the day is included in the price. The skyr cheesecake is very tasty.
✉ Baldursgata 14 ☎ 552 3939
🕐 Dinner

TJARNARBAKKINN (££–£££)
This romantic old-style restaurant is found upstairs in the old theatre, the coffee-coloured tin-clad building at the end of Tjörnin by the Town Hall. The fare is traditional and the setting is charming with lace and silver.
✉ Vonarstræti 3 ☎ 562 9700
🕐 Lunch and dinner

TVEIR FISKAR (££–£££)
A restaurant on the harbour front, and designed along the feng shui principle, so it can't go wrong. The interior may be minimalist but the taste is full-on, with the Chef of the Year 2003 Einar Geirsson specialising in Icelandic fish.
✉ Geirsgata 9 ☎ 511 3474
🕐 Lunch and dinner

VIÐ TJÖRNINA (£££)
The best restaurant in town for fish, you'll find it hidden down between the Tjörn and the Lutheran cathedral on the first floor of an unprepossessing place. It feels like you're walking into a favourite aunt's front parlour, with old lace, pretty china and home-made scrap menus. Marinaded cod-cheeks are the house speciality and taste infinitely better than they sound – highly recommended. Book ahead.
✉ Templarasund 3 ☎ 551 8666
🕐 Lunch and Dinner Mon–Sat; dinner only Sun

VIÐEY
VIÐEYJARSTOFA (£££)
Superb restaurant in a famous old historic house, and with the bonus of a lovely island setting. Catch the summer ferry from Reykjavík's new harbour.
✉ Viðey ☎ 562 1934
🕐 Afternoon tea and dinner

THE WEST
BLÁA LÓNIÐ (£–££)
The food in the restaurant at the Blue Lagoon is well worth stopping off for, with an à la carte menu and a full view over the lagoon itself.
✉ 5km from Grindavík ☎ 426 8800 🕐 Lunch and dinner

HAFNARFJÖRÐUR
FJÖRUKRÁIN (£–££)
Magnificent Viking-themed restaurant and bar by the harbour. The décor is bold, imaginative and beautifully observed; the atmosphere is eccentric and fun.
✉ Strandgata 55 ☎ 565 1213/565 1890 🕐 Lunch and dinner

NORTH AND NORTHWEST

AKUREYRI
BAUTINN (£–££)
This cheerful, no-frills restaurant occupies a great spot on the corner opposite the big book shop Bókval, with a conservatory dining room overlooking the main street. The house speciality is an excellent hamburger and chips, but you could try pasta with ham and mushrooms, or grilled salmon if you prefer. An Akureyri institution.
✉ Hafnarstræti 92 ☎ 462 1818
🕐 Lunch and dinner

BLÁA KANNAN (£)
Occupying one half of the magnificent old turreted building on Hafnarstræti, opposite Bókval bookstore

and handy for downtown shopping. Inside, the stylish café has something of a French air, with lots of pale wood, chandeliers and modern art on the walls. There's a great selection of cakes to consume with your coffee as well as quiches and sandwiches, ideal for a light lunch. A no smoking establishment.

✉ Hafnarstræti 96 ☎ 461 4600
🕐 Lunch and dinner

CAFÉ KARÓLÍNA (£–££)

Trendy café-cum-restaurant in Akureyri's stylish 'art' street, opposite the gallery of modern art.

✉ Kaupvangsstræti 23 ☎ 461 2755 🕐 Lunch and dinner

FIÐLARINN (££–£££)

Beautifully appointed and romantically lit modern restaurant overlooking the harbour area of Akureyri, with a wine bar in the lounge next door. International cuisine and extensive wine list.

✉ Skipagata 14 ☎ 462 7100
🕐 Lunch and dinner

GREIFINN (£)

Children are welcome at this large bronze-coloured restaurant near the town centre, a favourite with local families. You can get anything from burgers and Tex-Mex to sophisticated Italian-Icelandic fusion: try salted cod glazed with basil pesto, served with a cheese rissotto, garlic roasted vegetables and a tomato herb sauce.

✉ Glerárgötu 20 ☎ 460 1600

HÚSAVÍK
GAMLI BAUKUR (£–££)

In a modern timber building right on the harbour front, this lively restaurant is well placed for summer trade, spilling out onto the balcony on fine nights. Inside the woodwork is nautical and appealing, with old photos of Húsavík fishing boats. You can have anything

from a snack of a bacon and cheese sandwich and chips or perhaps deep-fried prawns with a sweet and sour sauce; or splash out and try the tenderloin of lamb with ginger sauce. Daily specials, a children's menu and a good wine list.

✉ On the harbour ☎ 464 2350
🕐 Lunch and dinner

SOUTH AND SOUTHEAST

BREIÐDALSVÍK
HÓTEL BLÁFELL (£–££)

Good food in restaurant of the timber hotel by the harbour. You can get home-made soup of the day or a toasted sandwich at lunchtime, or try shrimp cakes with sweet and sour sauce or smoked pork chops. Pizzas also served in the evenings.

✉ Sólvellir 14 ☎ 475 6770
🕐 Lunch and dinner

HÖFN
HAFNARBÚÐIN (£)

Höfn's very own drive-through hamburger takeaway and fast-food café, cheerfully painted in yellow and blue and right by the harbour. Open from 7:30AM to 11:30PM, winter and summer.

✉ Harbour front ☎ 478 1095
🕐 All day

KAFFI HORNIÐ (£–££)

Höfn's newest restaurant still looks a bit raw on the outside, but the timbering inside makes it light and airy. It's well placed on the main road to the harbour and the food is great. The menu has a bistro feel – you can have a grilled sandwich with ham, cheese and salad or, for something more substantial, the creamy pasta with lobster, bread and salad is excellent. There are good vegetarian choices, too, and a wide selection of beer and wine.

✉ Hafnarbraut 42 ☎ 478 2600
🕐 Lunch and dinner

On the road

On your travels you may find that, with such a small and scattered resident population, there are long distances between towns with restaurants. The network of petrol stations come to the rescue here, acting not only as essential toilet stops, but always with a pot of hot coffee on tap and usually offering a range of other snacks, including the ubiquitous hotdogs. And amongst the household-name chocolate bars, you'll discover liquorice in every conceivable form – very much a local favourite.

Hotels & Guest Houses

Prices

Approximate price for a double room for one night

£ = under 5,000ISK
££ = 5,000–8,000ISK
£££ = over 8,000ISK

Note that prices fluctuate hugely according to high and low season.

Farm Stays

For comfortable (if sometimes rather basic) budget accomodation, Icelandic Farm Holidays offers around 130 possibilities all over the country, ranging from simple bed and breakfast on working farms to more elaborate farmstead hotels with a full range of guest facilities. Accommodation is graded and inspected, and can be booked centrally from the helpful Reykjavik office. If you don't want to plan too far ahead, you can pre-purchase vouchers for a minimum of five nights from any tour operator and simply book ahead 24-hours in advance. IFH Tours ✉ Siðumúli 13, Reykjavík ☎ 570 2700; www.farmholidays.is

Guest Houses

Usually offer a good basic standard of accommodation in main towns and tourist centres, with shared facilities such as bathroom and kitchen, and often cheaper if you bring your own sleeping-bag. Breakfast is usually charged as a separate option and it's useful to travel with your own supplies of tea and coffee.

REYKJAVÍK

BALDURSBRÁ (£–££)

Friendly guest house offering comfortable and spacious bed and breakfast accommodation in a quiet quarter within a few minutes' walk of the town centre. Proprietors Joachim and Ariane Fischer are funds of local knowledge. Free transfer available to and from airport bus.
✉ Laufásvegur 41 ☎ 552 6646
🕐 All year

HÓLL COTTAGE (£££)

This lovely historic cottage on a side street in the centre of town offers you a quiet space to call your own within easy walking distance of all the main attractions. Beautifully restored and thoughtfully equipped, sleeps 4–6, self-catering.
✉ Grjótagata 12 ☎ 562 3614
🕐 All year

HÓTEL BORG (£££)

Iceland's oldest and smartest hotel, recently restored to 1930s art deco splendour, and complete with ballroom. Every bedroom is decorated with a different theme and equipped with its own CD player (borrow discs from reception).
✉ Pósthússtræti 11 ☎ 551 1440 🕐 All year

HÓTEL HOLT (£££)

A stylish and luxurious modern hotel set discreetly amid the international embassies in a gracious part of the town centre. Boasts a fine restaurant, as well as modern art on every wall.
✉ Bergstaðastræti 37
☎ 552 5700 🕐 All year

THE WEST

BORGARNES

BJARG (£–££)

Comfortable bed and breakfast accommodation in a splendid old gabled farmhouse outside the town, good walking in the area.
✉ By Borgarnes ☎ 437 1925
🕐 All year

LÁTRABJARG

BREIÐAVÍK (£–££)

Simple bed and breakfast accommodation in a renovated former schoolhouse. Convenient for exploring the bird cliffs, and offers fishing permits for the local lakes.
✉ Látrabjarg ☎ 456 1575
🕐 May–Sep

SNÆFELLSNES

GUESTHOUSE BREKKUBÆR (£–££)

Pleasant bed and breakfast accommodation, with optional meditation, in the community at Hellnar, just around the coast from Arnarstapi. Lots of good walking in the area as well as access to Snæfellsjökull.
✉ Hellnar ☎ 435 6820 🕐 All year, but advance booking required Oct–May

GUESTHOUSE LANGAHOLT (£–££)

You're guaranteed a friendly welcome at this family hotel, in a fantastic setting on a long sandy beach with its own 9-hole golf course and views to the Snæfell glacier. Variety of rooms and facilities available, from sleeping-bag to a high standard of comfort with your own bathroom.
✉ Garðar ☎ 435 6719/435 6789
🕐 Mar–Nov

NORTH AND NORTHWEST

AKUREYRI

HÓTEL KEA (££–£££)

A very pleasant modern hotel at the foot of the steps to the cathdral, and in the heart of the old town. All rooms have private shower, TV and mini-bar, and there's an impressive restaurant.
✉ Hafnarstræti 87–89 ☎ 460 2000 🕔 All year

SALKA GUESTHOUSE (£)

Clean and pleasant self-catering apartment with three bedrooms, shared bathroom and kitchen. It's very conveniently set in the middle of downtown Akureyri but can get noisy at weekends (earplugs thoughtfully provided!).
✉ Skipagata 1 ☎ 461 2340 🕔 All year

HÚSAVÍK

FOSSHÓTEL HÚSAVÍK (££–£££)

What the décor may lack in modernity is more than made up for by the warm welcome you'll receive here – it's the friendliest hotel in Iceland, and with a great restaurant too. It's tucked up behind the Norwegian church, so central but quiet.
✉ Ketilsbraut 22 ☎ 464 1220 🕔 All year

MIÐFJÖRÐUR

BREKKULÆKUR (£–££)

Comfortable bed and breakfast accommodation (dinner on request) on a horse ranch, in a peaceful location in a broad green valley, handy for exploring the north coast. Specialises in guided trekking, both long- and short-distance, but also wildlife and hiking tours.
✉ Hvammstangi ☎ 451 2938 🕔 All year, including Christmas, but advance booking required Sep–May

MÝVATN

SEL-LYKILHÓTEL MÝVATN (££–£££)

A modern and comfortable hotel on Route 1, in a quiet area to the south of Reykjalíð, overlooking the lake.
✉ Skútustaðir ☎ 464 4164 🕔 Summer only

SOUTH AND SOUTHEAST

EGILSSTAÐIR

GISTIHÚSIÐ EGILSSTÖDUM (£–££)

Beautiful old house, away from the main road and overlooking the lake. Bedrooms are fresh and comfortable, the welcome friendly.
✉ Egilsstaðir ☎ 471 1114 🕔 All year

HÖFN

ÁRNANES (£–££)

A comfortable modern complex outside town, close to the local airport (not busy). Accommodation is in five wooden houses and there's a good restaurant on site.
✉ 781 Hornafjörður ☎ 478 1550 🕔 Lunch and dinner

HÓTEL HÖFN (££–£££)

An IcelandAir hotel of comfortable international standard just on the edge of the town centre, with good views. The restaurant on the upper floor serves a seafood smorgasbord on summer evenings. Bedrooms have their own TV and bathroom.
✉ Víkurbraut 24 ☎ 478 1240 🕔 All year

MÝRDALUR

SÓLHEIMAHJÁLEIGA (£)

Simple bed and breakfast accommodation is offered in this old farmhouse, with shared facilities and a great view from the ground-level kitchen window. Sheep, cows and horses on the farm.
✉ Mýrdalur ☎ 467 1320 🕔 All year

Edda Hotels

This chain offers a range of good value accommodation, from bring-your-own sleeping-bag upwards, and occupies the comfortable modern boarding houses for schools around the country through the summer holidays, Jun–Aug. They all offer restaurant facilities and most are near a swimming pool. ☎ 505 0910 for further information; www.hoteledda.is.

Youth Hostels

There are 26 of these around Iceland, offering budget accommodation for families, complete with duvets – bring your own sheets. Check out the deals for overnight vouchers combined with bus passports or car rental. The hostels quickly fill up in summer, so book ahead.
✉ Icelandic Youth Hostel Association, Sundlaugavegur 34, 105 Reykjavík ☎ 553 8110; www.hostel.is

Shopping

Tax-free Shopping

Visitors are entitled to reclaim 15 per cent on purchases of more than 4000ISK made at any shop displaying the 'tax-free' symbol. You pay the full price at the checkout, but ask and you'll be given a form to fill in. Hand this in at the airport bank when you leave showing the goods as proof, to obtain your refund – the saving is well worth it. You do not have to show woollen goods in this way.

Christmas Every Day

Don't miss Jólagarðinn, the red-painted house where it's Christmas every day, just out beyond Kjarnaskógar – stuffed with beautiful Christmas items, including traditional Icelandic decorations, it's brilliant, and you can picnic in the garden. A whimsical wishing tree and fairytale tower were added in 2003.

Laugavegur is **Reykjavík**'s famous shopping street, with lots of high-class designer fashion, hand-crafted jewellery, two great book stores (with books and magazines in all languages, not just Icelandic), and small cafés. Several shops cater exclusively for babies and toddler fashion – cute, but not cheap. For grown-up fashion, Pelsinn, beside the Domkirkjan, has a stylish range. More exclusive designer clothes, jewellery, and art and antiques shops are found on Skólavörðustígur.

Elsewhere, for Icelandic crafts try the Rammagerðin gift shop on Laugarvegur and Hafnarstræti, which stocks treasures from designer glassware to handmade wooden toys; the Traveller Shop on Barkarstræti for maps, guides and novelties; and for gifts, jewellery and top-class woollens, historic Thorvaldsens Bazar (on the corner of Aðalstræti and Austurstræti) has a great selection – shop profits have supported children's charities for years. For top value, Álafoss, north of town in Mosfellsbær, is a factory outlet with woollens and other souvenirs, including beautiful blankets, ceramics and glassware, and offering quality at discount prices.

Kringlan is the city's showpiece shopping mall, with more than 100 outlets – you can buy anything here from classy Swedish homeware to modern art. It's set away from the town centre but with a free car park underneath, and easy bus access. The latest trendy fashions include Noa Noa and Karen Millen, as well as the department store Hagkaup. For outdoor and camping gear you won't beat the vast Nanoq store, complete with artificial stream and climbing wall. Íslandia sells a wides range of souvenirs, from knitwear to lava candle-holders. The upper floor has a choice of fast food outlets, including a Hard Rock Café. The new Smárland shopping mall in Kópavogur, a few miles from the city centre, includes some good boutiques among its more ordinary shops and international names such as Debenhams and Benetton.

If you want to take some Icelandic delicacies home with you, try the little market in Kolaportið, on Tryggvagata – it has everything from pancakes to great sides of smoked salmon, and you can often taste before you buy.

Akureyri also offers good shopping, though on a smaller scale. The main shopping street is pedestrianised Hafnarstræti, with the famous Bókval book and audio store on the corner. Fold-Anna is a factory outlet for beautiful woollen goods, including capes, blankets and hats. Skrautla gallerí stocks some unusual and quality crafts, and ceramics and art prints are found at Listfléttan. For souvenirs, the Viking shop has a good range, and Gallerí Grúska, on Strandgata, is staffed by and for local artisans, with unusual handmade items such as fish-skin jewellery and eccentric hats. High fashion is found along Skipagata, with trendy designer outlets such as Perfect. Gleratorg is the town's shopping mall.

Children's Attractions

REYKJAVÍK PARK AND ZOO, REYKJAVÍK

A lively summer theme park and play area on a Viking theme, with an informal zoo including local species such as Icelandic horses, Arctic foxes and reindeer. A variety of activities for older kids including electric cars and diggers. On-site café, toilets and changing facilities. Admission free for holders of City Tourist Card. Great swimming pool close by.
✉ Laugardalur park ☎ 575 7800; www.mu.is

THE VOLCANO SHOW, REYKJAVÍK

Daily film shows of errupting vocanoes and earthquakes make a great introduction to the geology and landscape of Iceland. Shows in English and other languages, all year round, in the Red Rock Cinema near Hótel Holt.
✉ Hellsundi 6a ☎ 551 3230/552 2539

PUFFIN ISLAND CRUISE, REYKJAVÍK

Around 10 million puffins spend the late spring and summer in Iceland. These little birds, with their colourful red and blue bills and stubby wings, nest in burrows on Lundey, a low green island accessible from Reykjavik on a 1½-hour boat trip.
🚢 Viðey-Ferry from Sundahöfn at 4:45 ☎ 581 1010

HAFNARFJÖRÐUR

Rapidly developing as the Viking capital of Iceland, Hafnarfjörður boasts not only a fantastic Viking restaurant on the harbour front, including some life-sized models outside and a fascinating interior, but also an entire Viking 'village', where crafsmen can be seen at work in the West Nordic Cultural House. And if your children are into the mysteries of elves, there are popular guided walks around the elf settlements of the town, when who knows what you might see?. For details, contact the Tourist Information Office at Vesturgata 8, ☎ 565 0661.

SAFNASAFRID, AKUREYRI

The Icelandic Folk Art Museum lies 12km north of Akureyri, and contains a whacky collection of colourful folk art pieces, from wooden cats to characterful dolls, toys and unusual sculpture.
✉ Svalbarðsströnd ☎ 461 4066 🕐 May–Sep, daily 10–6

HVALAMIÐSTÖÐIN (WHALE MUSEUM), HÚSAVÍK

This is a great place for children hoping to see whales and dolphins, with good pictorial information to identify the main species, real whale-skeletons so you get an idea of their size, and an amazing 'touch table' where you can compare the feel of whale-skin and shark-skin. A whole corner is dedicated to Keiko, killer-whale star of the children's film *Free Willy*, including a life-size model.
✉ Hafnarstétt ☎ 464 2520

THE SANDGERÐI NATURE CENTRE, SANDGERÐI

This popular centre on the western tip of Reykjanes promises 'instruction, exhibits, fun and adventure on land and sea', with everything from sailing to story-telling.
✉ Garðvegur 1 ☎ 423 7551/897 8007

Reykjavík Tourist Card

The Reykjavík Tourist Card is available from the Tourist Information Centre in Reyjavík, the City Hall Information Desk, hotels and guest houses, BSÍ coach terminal, museums and outdoor thermal pools. It is valid for one to three days and allows unlimited travel on Reykjavik city buses, admission to seven outdoor thermal pools, and attractions including the National Art Gallery, the Ásmundur Jónsson Collection, Reykjavik Art Museum and the Familiy Park and Reykjavík Zoo. Prices:
24 hours – 1,000ISK;
48 hours – 1,500ISK;
72 hours – 2,000ISK.

Patronymics

People are widely called by their given first name in Iceland, from the Prime Minister down. Children take their father's name as their surname, adding 'son' or 'daughter' at the end, and this is kept for life. For example, in one family husband and wife Jón Arnarson and Svava Stefánsdóttir could have two children, a boy and a girl, Magnús Jónsson and Erla Jónsdóttir. Not surprisingly, therefore, you'll find the phone book is alphabetically organised by first names.

Nightlife and the Arts

Get on the Net

A growing number of cafés in Reykjavík offer internet access. Try the Ráðhúskaffi in the town hall, by the Tjöra, Netkaffi 524 at Kringlan shopping mall, or Deli on Bankastræti. You can also go on-line at the Reykjavík Travel Service information centre on Lækjargata, and at the BSI bus terminal on Vatnsmýravegur.

REYKJAVÍK

Live Arts

NATIONAL THEATRE
Quality drama, the place to see Shakespeare performed in Icelandic.
✉ Hverfisgata ☎ 551 1200

REYKJAVÍK CITY THEATRE
Lively performances of dance, theatre and musicals, as well as touring productions.
✉ Listabraut 3 ☎ 568 8000

ICELAND OPERA
The national opera company boasts the northernmost opera house in the world. Limited performances in summer.
✉ Ingólfstræti ☎ 511 6400/4200

ICELAND SYMPHONY ORCHESTRA
The Iceland Symphony Orchestra is world-class, offering international programmes throughout the year along with a wide range of recordings too. Catch it if you can.
✉ Háskólabíó ☎ 545 2500

SALURINN, KÓPAVOGUR
Iceland's first purpose-built concert hall hosts a wide range of music from chamber music to jazz.
✉ Hamraborg ☎ 554 4501/570 0400

Cinema
Reykjavík has several cinemas showing films in their original language with Icelandic sub-titles.
✉ Sambia, Álfabakki 8
☎ 587 8900
✉ Sambia, Kringlan
☎ 588 0800
✉ Laugarásbíó, Laugarás

☎ 553 2075
✉ Regnboginn, Hverfisgata 54
☎ 551 9000
✉ Smarabia, Smáralind, Kópavogur ☎ 564 0000

Nightlife
In Reykjavík and other main centres, innocent cafés by day turn into pubs and clubs at night, and the capital is getting an international reputation for the quality and variety of night-time entertainment on offer. Friday and Saturday are the big nights out, but be aware that nothing serious starts before 11PM. Fashions change and what's 'in' one month may be *passé* the next, but here are some current recommendations.

BROADWAY
Just out of the town centre, this disco in Hótel Ísland is said to be the biggest in Iceland. Live music and cabaret.
✉ Ármúli 9 ☎ 533 1100

KAFFI SÓLON
Restaurant and gallery by day, bar by night, where the arty crowd hang out.
✉ Bankastræti 7a ☎ 562 3232

THE DUBLINER
Every city has its Irish theme pub these days, and why should Reykjavík be the exception? Locals say it was imported from the Emerald Isle (complete with staff) on the back of a lorry.
✉ Hafnarstræti 4 ☎ 511 3233

GAUKUR Á STÖNG
The oldest pub in town, offering live music most evenings.
✉ Tryggvagata 22 ☎ 551 1556

GLAUMBAR
If you like your music loud, then this sporty bar near the old harbour is for you.
✉ Tryggvagata 22 ☎ 552 868

HVERFISBARINN
Located at the National Theatre, this is a café by day and lively bar in the evening.
✉ Hverfisgata 20 ☎ 511 6700

KAFFI LIST
Spanish-themed café and bar, with Latin American music at weekends.
✉ Laugavegur 20a ☎ 562 5059

KAFFI REYKJAVÍK
A good pub atmosphere in a large old building near the harbour. Dancing and live music at weekends.
✉ Vesturgata 2 ☎ 562 5540

KAFFIBARINN
A trendy spot for posers and wannabes. Between the Hallgrímskirkja and the Tjörn.
✉ Bergstaðastraeti 1 ☎ 551 1588

NASA
Bills itself as the biggest nightclub in the centre of the capital, popular with all ages.
✉ Austurvöllur ☎ 511 1313

PIANO BAR
Intimate piano bar on the first floor of one of Reykjavík's oldest houses.
✉ Laekjartorg Square ☎ 562 4045

SIRKUS
Ever-popular wine bar and nightclub, just off Laugavegur, with a great choice of wines by the glass.
✉ Klapparstígur 31 ☎ 511 8022

SKUGGABARINN
In the smart Hótel Borg, this is where the well-dressed dance the night away.
✉ Pósthusstraeti 11 ☎ 551 1440

SPOTLIGHT
The centre of Reykjavík's gay scene promises wild music and dancing.
✉ Hafnarstraeti 17 ☎ 562 6813

VEGAMÓT
Bistro and bar off Laugavegur, great for sitting and talking if the dance scene is not your thing.
✉ Vegemótastígur ☎ 511 3040

AKUREYRI
Iceland's second city is busy building up its own nightlife, though it can't compete with the capital.

Theatre

LEIKFÉLAG AKUREYRAR
The only professional company outside Reykjavík, in historic theatre building.
✉ Hafnarstraeti 57 ☎ 462 5073

LISTASUMAR
Organises summer arts programmes of concerts, jazz and cultural events.
✉ Kaupvangsstraeti 23 ☎ 461 2609

Cinemas
✉ Borgarbió, Hólabraut 12 ☎ 462 3500
✉ Nýja-Bíó, Ráðhústorgi 2 ☎ 461 4666

Nightlife

GRAENI HATTURINN
Extensive bar below the Blaa Kánnan café, popular with all ages. Entrance via the café or from the side.
✉ Hafnarstraeti 96 ☎ 461 4646

KAFFI AKUREYRI
Evening bar, with live music at weekends, popular with younger crowd. Café by day.
✉ Strandgata 7 ☎ 461 3999

SJALLINN
Lively pub and nightclub, with live bands at weekends. Great atmosphere. Over 18s.
✉ Geislagata 14 ☎ 462 2770

Getting in
Most bars and nightspots offer free entry before midnight, but you may have to queue. Alcohol is very expensive, so locals tend to drink at home before coming out, and are raring to go when they do. There's not much action before 11PM but nobody goes home before 4–5AM either.

Sport & Leisure

Gone to the dogs
For something different, try a ride on a sledge pulled by Iceland's only team of huskies. The dogs are from Greenland stock, very strong, and liable to lick you all over. The operation is run by Denis and Berglind Pedersen of Dog Steam Tours, Bolholt, 851 Hella ☎ 487 7747; www.dogsledding.is

Aerial Sightseeing

For a bird's-eye view of volcanoes and glaciers, Íslandsflug offer special sightseeing flights in small aircraft, flying from the airport in the centre of Reykjavík. Iceland's clear air means visibility can be pin-sharp, and if weather conditions are right, it's a great way to get an overview of the country. Contact Íslandsflug ☎ 570 8030.

Birdwatching

The concentration of nesting birds in Iceland makes it paradise for birdwatchers. The main season for migrants is mid-May to mid-Aug, and two of the best places to see them are Mývatn and Látrabjarg (► 19, 45). If you're serious, it's worth going with a specialist tour operator, such as Naturetrek ✉ Cheriton Mill, Cheriton, Alresford, Hampshire SO24 0NG ☎ 01962 733051.

Cycling

Cycling around Iceland can be a bit of a challenge, with bumpy and unmade roads, and unpredictable weather. Sandstorms can be a hazard in the south. Still, in an eco-friendly country, people like to do it. Contact local tourist offices for information about cycle hire, and if you bring your own, bring plenty of spares. The Icelandic Mountainbike Club (ÍFHK) has information to help you plan your trip, and a friendly club which meets Thu PM at Brekkustígur 2, Reykjavík. Contact them at PO Box 1593, 125 Reykjavík ☎ 562 0099, www.mmedia.is/~ifhk/tourist.htm

Dolphin- and Whale-Spotting

Several sites around Iceland offer facilities for this, and Húsavík is probably the best – contact Norður-Sigling, PO Box 122, 640 Húsavík, ☎ 464 2350. It also offers good information to back up what you see at the Whale Museum, Hafnarstétt ☎ 464 2520, with help to identify the main species, real skeletons to give an idea of their size, and an excellent collecton of reference books. Whale Safari in Reykjavík (☎ 533 2660), MS *Moby Dick* in Keflavík (☎ 421 7777), Sæferðir in Stykkishólmur (☎ 438 1450) and Sjóferðir Sea Tours in Dalvík (☎ 466 3355) offer similar trips.

Fishing

With over 100 salmon rivers, 20 of them world-ranked, Iceland offers great sport fishing from mid-Jun to mid-Sep; but the best places are not cheap. Contact tourist information centres about opportunities and permits, or The National Angling Association, Bolholt 6, 105 Reykjavík (☎ 553 1510). Sea angling trips are possible from some harbours – Angling Club Lax-á (☎ 557 6100) and Sjóferðir Sea-Tours in Dalvík (☎ 466 3355) offer information.

Hiking

For many visitors, this is what Iceland's all about, and there's good local information and mapping to help you plan your routes. The terrain, particularly in the interior, can be harsh, and weather conditions change very quickly, so seek expert advice on the correct equipment depending on your route and time of travel. The land is fragile, and so camping outside official sites is discouraged, but there are over 100 campsites offering a range of facilities – for listings, contact the tourist information centre, Reykjavík. There is also a good network of huts around the best walking areas – contact the Touring Club of Iceland (Ferðafélag Íslands), Mörkinni 6, 108 Reykjavík ☎ 568 2533, e-mail: fi@fi.is. They also offer a programme of organized walks throughout the year. Also Mountain Guides, for guided walks and ice climbing, Vagnhöfða 7b, 110 Reykjavík ☎ 587 9999/894 2959; www.mountainguide.is

Horse-riding

A must for any rider and well worth a try even if you've never been on horseback before. The horses are small, surefooted and very comfortable to ride. The 'fifth gait' with head held high, unique to Icelandic horses, is much smoother than a bumpy trot and not as fast as a rollicking canter. Treks can be arranged to suit any ability and get you out into the wilds. Recommended: Íshestar Riding Tours, Sörlaskeið 26, 220 Hafnarfjörður ☎ 555 7000. Skipalækur, Fellabær, by Egilsstaðr ☎ 471 1324. Brekkulækur, 531 Hvammstangi ☎ 451 2938.

River Rafting

This popular sport is growing in Iceland, which has no shortage of good rivers offering adventures of varying thrills and spills. For details contact Ævintýraferðir Activity Tours, PO Box 75, 560 Varmahlið ☎ 453 8383; www.rafting.is; or Arctic Rafting at Árnes ☎ 568 3030, www.arcticrafting.is

Swimming

A ready supply of cheap hot water means that Iceland boasts more outdoor public swimming pools per head than the rest of Europe put together. The standard is high, entry prices low and there are often bubbling 'hot-pots' and water-chutes. Akureyri boasts one of the finest, but you'll find them in just about every town and settlement, often open until 8 or 9PM.

Winter Sports

There's not enough good snow for a lot of top-class skiing in Iceland, but the best is found in the north around Akureyri, which also has a new skating rink. Skidoos offer transport over the snowcaps all year round and trips are available around all the main glaciers. The snowmobiles are easy to operate and fun, if rather noisy and smelly, and can get you high into the wilds quickly – but stick close to your guide as there is a real danger of crevasses, especially in the summer. Warm overalls and helmets are provided. Driving over the snow in vehicles with vastly outsized tyres, called 'big foot' or 'monster trucks', is also popular. For advice on the best packages, contact the Central Reykjavík Travel Service at Læljargate 2, Reykjavík ☎ 511 2442; www.travelservice.is

Golf

This is Iceland's fastest growing sport and you'll find 9-hole courses everywhere. For a round on the best 18-hole courses, contact the clubs at:
Reykjavík (two championship courses), ☎ 587 2211
Akureyri ☎ 462 2974
Keflavík ☎ 421 4100
Hafnarfjörður ☎ 565 3360
Westmann Islands ☎ 481 2363

What's On When

Yuletide Lads

Christmas for children in Iceland has its own very special dimension. According to tradition, 13 boisterous 'Yuletide lads' come to call, one each night leading up to 25 December, to leave a small gift in the child's shoe placed in a window for that purpose. (If the child has been naughty, there'll be a potato in there in the morning instead.) The lads are pranksters and nicknamed accordingly – 'Sausage Snatcher', 'Door Slammer', 'Candle Snuffer' and so on – and they are ruled over by a fearsome matriarch called Gryla, who eats bad children for breakfast. She has a big black cat, who'll also eat you if you have no new clothes to wear on Christmas Day.

1 January

New Year: Celebrations start the afternoon before – a great excuse for bonfires and fireworks.

6 January

Twelfth Night: More bonfires and fireworks to brighten up the long dark nights.

Late January to late February

Thorrablót: Celebration of traditional winter foods, with the eating of delicacies such as whey-pickled fish and rams' testicles, washed down with *brennivín*.

April

Shrove Tuesday: 'Bursting Day' (Sprengidalur) is commemorated by feasting on lamb and pea soup. The previous Monday is 'Bun Day' (Bolludagur), when children go round threatening to beat the grown-ups with sticks, and demanding buns. *Easter*: Everything closes from Maundy Thursday to Easter Monday. On Ash Wednesday (Óskudagur), children attempt to hang little bags of ashes on the backs of unsuspecting adults.

Around 20 April

First Day of Summer (Sumardagurinn fyrsti): An important landmark Thursday celebrated in carnival style.

Early June

Seamen's Day (Sjómannadagurinn) : Harbours are filled with ships and vessels of all sizes on this Sunday, and celebrations include rowing races and tugs of war.

17 June

National Day (Thjóðhátíð): Carnival-type festivities are held all over Iceland.

Late June

The Arctic Open: This cheerful four-day golf championship, open to professionals and amateurs, is played through the light summer nights on the world's most northerly golf course. At Akureyri, it lies 65° 40' north of the Equator. *International Viking Festival*: Held every two years or so (the Fifth was celebrated in 2003), this is an unmissable Viking jamboree of singing, dancing, eating and fighting in the best traditions, held in Hafnarfjörður.

Early July

Höfn Lobster Festival (Hátíð á Höfn): A big party with music, dance, competitions and feasting.

First weekend in August

Herring Festival (Síldaraevintri): Extensive celebrations with eating, drinking and dancing in Siglufjorður, former herring capital of Iceland.

Early August

Westmann Islands Festival (Thjóðhátíð): Independence Day party, held on Heimaey, with barbecues, bonfires and roistering.

September

Reltir: Round-ups on horseback are held all over the country, bringing sheep and horses down from the hills before winter sets in.

23 December

Thorláksmessa: Celebrated in the best restaurants by the eating of cured skate.

24–5 December

Christmas starts officially at noon on 24th, and presents are given that day.

Practical Matters

Above: a 4WD in trouble in a fast flowing glacial river
Right: a sign warns of road conditions ahead, where 4WD will be needed to get through the rivers

TIME DIFFERENCES

GMT	Iceland	USA (NY)	Germany	Netherlands	Spain
12 noon	12 noon	← 7AM	→ 1PM	→ 1PM	→ 1PM

BEFORE YOU GO

WHAT YOU NEED

● Required ○ Suggested ▲ Not required	Some countries require a passport to remain valid for a minimum period (usually at least six months) beyond the date of entry – contact their consulate or embassy or your travel agent for details.	UK	Germany	USA	Netherlands	Spain
Passport		●	●	●	●	●
Visa (regulations can change – check before planning your journey)		▲	▲	▲	▲	▲
Onward or Return Ticket		▲	▲	▲	▲	▲
Health Inoculations		▲	▲	▲	▲	▲
Health Documentation		▲	▲	▲	▲	▲
Travel Insurance		●	●	●	●	●
Driving Licence (national)		●	●	●	●	●
Car Insurance Certificate (if own car)		●	●	●	●	●
Car Registration Document (if own car)		●	●	●	●	●

WHEN TO GO

Iceland (for a weather forecast in English ☎ 902 0600-44, summer only)

▬▬▬ High season

☐ Low season

0.5°C	-1°C	-1.4°C	4°C	6.6°C	10.1°C	11.1°C	11.3°C	8.3°C	2.9°C	2.2°C	1.2°C
JAN	FEB	MAR	APR	MAY	JUN	JUL	AUG	SEP	OCT	NOV	DEC
🌧	🌧	🌧	☁	⛅	⛅	☀	⛅	☁	☁	🌧	🌧

🌧 Wet   ☁ Cloud   ⛅ Sun/showers   ☀ Sun

TOURIST OFFICES

In the UK
IcelandAir
172 Tottenham Court Road,
3rd floor
London W1P OLY
☎ (0207) 874 1000
Fax: (0207) 387 5711

In the USA
Icelandic Tourist Board
655 Third Avenue
New York NY 10017
☎ (212) 885 9700
Fax: (212) 885 9710

In the Netherlands
IcelandAir
Muntplein 2
NL-1012 WR Amsterdam
☎ (020) 627 0136
Fax: (020) 623 8010

CONSULATES

UK
Laufásvegur 31,
Reykjavík 550 5100

Germany
Laufásvegur 31,
Reykjavík 530 1100

USA
Laufásvegur 21,
Reykjavík 562 9100

WHEN YOU ARE THERE

ARRIVING

Iceland express connects daily with London and Copenhagen. Icelandair is the chief operator of international flights, flying from London, Glasgow, Copenhagen, Oslo, Paris, Stockholm, Amsterdam, Hamburg, Frankfurt, Zurich, Barcelona, Madrid, Milan, Boston, New York, Baltimore, Orlando and Minneapolis. A regular shuttle bus operates between Keflavík airport and Reykjavík. Bus transport to Keflavík airport from Icelandair Hótel Loftleiðir about 2½ hours before departure ☎ 562 1011.

MONEY

The monetary unit of Iceland is the króna (Ik), plural krónur. Notes are in denominations of 500, 1000, 2000 and 5000, and coins of 1, 5, 10, 50, 100. Foreign currencies and travellers' cheques can be exchanged at all banks, savings banks and bureaux de change. Credit cards are widely used and accepted in most places. Visa, MasterCard and JCB credit cards are widely accepted, as are the debit cards Visa, Electron, Maestro and EDC.

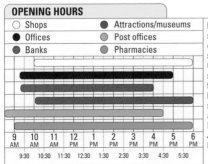

CUSTOMS

YES
Goods Obtained Duty Free (Limits):
Alcohol (under 47% vol): 1L and Alcohol (under 21% vol): 1 L or Imported beer 6L or Icelandic beer 8L
Cigarettes 200, or the equivalent of other tobacco products. Up to three times the duty-free allowance for tobacco and alcohol may be brought into the country, subject to declaration at Customs and the payment of all additional Icelandic dues on them. **You must be over 20 to benefit from alcohol allowances, and over 16 for the tobacco allowances.**
Visitors are allowed to bring food into the country duty-free, with a limit of 10kg or ISK4,000 per person.

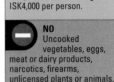

NO
Uncooked vegetables, eggs, meat or dairy products, narcotics, firearms, unlicensed plants or animals.

OPENING HOURS

○ Shops	● Attractions/museums
● Offices	○ Post offices
● Banks	○ Pharmacies

9 AM	10 AM	11 AM	12 PM	1 PM	2 PM	3 PM	4 PM	5 PM	6 PM
9:30	10:30	11:30	12:30	1:30	2:30	3:30	4:30	5:30	

Most shops are open for a shorter time on Saturday, often closing at 4 or earlier, but may stay open until 7 on Fridays. Office hours may be earlier in summer. Banks may stay open for longer on Thursdays and Fridays. Money exchange services in Reykjavík are available at the Tourist Information Centre, Aðalstræti 2, Jun–Aug, daily 8:30–6; Sep–May, Mon–Fri 9–1 and 2–5, Sat 10–2.

POLICE 112

FIRE 112

AMBULANCE 112

DRIVE ON THE
RIGHT

TOILETS
FREE

DRIVING

 Speed limit on main tarmac roads: 90kph

 Speed limit on main gravel roads: 80kph

 Speed limit in populated areas: 30/50kph

 Mandatory in front and rear seats

 The limit is 5 micrograms of alcohol in 100ml of breath and the penalties are severe – don't drink and drive

 Unleaded petrol is available as 95 octane (regular) and 98 octane (super). Filling stations around Reykjavík are open daily 7:30AM–8PM or later; around the country, times may vary, and some are open only in summer. Some filling stations have automats which take 500kr, 1000kr, 2000kr notes and credit and debit cards after hours, but these do not always work. Petrol stations can be few and far between, so don't let your fuel run low.

 In case of breakdown, telephone your hire car company or ☎ 5112 112 for emergency assistance. (The Icelandic motoring organisation AET has reciprocal agreements with AAA and European clubs such as AA.)

PUBLIC TRANSPORT

 Internal Flights Flugfélag Íslands (Air Iceland ☎ 570 3030) is the main operator of domestic flights and flights to the Faroes and Greenland, out of Reykjavík; Mýflug (☎ 464 4400) operates sightseeing flights from Mývatn.

 Buses Reykjavík's main BSÍ coach terminal is at Vatnsmýrarvegur 10, ☎ 591 1020. There are regular daily coach services around the country, including through the winter, and you can buy good value 'passport' tickets if you intend to travel widely on the network.

 Ferries The weekly car ferry from Denmark to Seyðisfjörður calls at Shetland, the Faroes and Norway. Contact Smyril Line Ísland, Laugavegur 3, 101 Reykjavík, ☎ 562 6362; e-mail: smyril-iceland@isholf.is. Local ferries operate between the mainland and main islands or remote areas, with extra sailings in summer.
Viðey ☎ 892 0099/581 1010
Flatey ☎ 438 1450
Hrísey ☎ 466 1797/852 2211
Westmann Islands ☎ 481 2800

 Urban Transport Reykjavík's yellow city buses operate from Hlemmur, at the eastern end of Laugavegur, or the central Lækjartorg square. They operate 7AM–12PM Mon–Sat, and 10AM–12PM Sun; some weekend buses run until 4AM. The fare is standard 220kr for adults (reduced for teenagers/children) and you need exact money for the ticket machine; alternatively, buy a book of tickets in advance and pay less. If you have to change buses on your journey, buy a *skiptimiða* (transfer ticket) from the driver, and you'll still pay only 220k.

CAR RENTAL

 Car hire is expensive so shop for the best deal – you may be able to combine with a fly-drive or farm-stay package, for example. A 4WD is essential if you plan going off the main roads. Check the cover – hire companies may not insure you on some routes.

TAXIS

 Widely available, many offer personalised taxi tours at fixed prices.
Hreyfill ☎ 588 5522
Borgarbíll ☎ 552 2440
BSR ☎ 561 0000
Bæjarleiðir ☎ 553 3500

PHOTOGRAPHY

What to photograph: sweeping views, mountainous landscapes, picturesque old cottages, fishing boats, rainbows and waterfalls, Icelandic horses, glaciers. You'll need expert lenses for the birds and wildlife.
When to photograph: whenever the sun shines!
Where to buy film: the most popular brands are widely available, but like everything else, may be more expensive than back home.

MOTORING INFORMATION

Driving Conditions On roundabouts, cars on the inside lane have right of way. Most of Route 1 is now tarmac but other roads are often unsurfaced gravel. Be prepared to slow right down when passing other vehicles, as loose gravel can be thrown up and road edges are soft; be cautious at narrow bridges and blind summits, and be prepared to give way (flashing headlights usually mean 'I'm coming through'). Stay on the roads and tracks. The natural environment is fragile and off-road driving carries heavy fines. Headlights must be switched on at all times when driving, day and night.

Driving in the Interior Many roads across central Iceland are only open for a few weeks in high summer, as weather conditions can change very quickly. If you're planning a trip, consult tourist information and locals before you set out and be especially cautious at unbridged rivers.

Animals Note that sheep, horses and cattle may stray onto the roads and you are liable to pay compensation for any animal injured or killed. Farm dogs chasing cars can be a particular hazard.

HEALTH

Doctors Visitors from the EU are entitled to reciprocal state medical care and should take form E111 which covers basic treatment. Citizens from elsewhere will need medical insurance. Note that extra medical insurance will not necessarily cover you for all activities. There is a 24-hour emergency ward at The National Hospital, Fossvogur ☎ 525 1700. Doctors are on duty in the evenings and at weekends at The Medical Center, Smáratorg 1, Kópavogur, near Reykjavík ☎ 554 0400.

Dental Services Ask at your hotel or guest house for details of local English-speaking dentists. An emergency number for weekend cover in Reykjavík is ☎ 575 0505.

Drugs Most pharmacies (Apótek) have English-speaking staff. For information on 24-hour opening ☎ 118.

Safe Water Cold tap water is some of the cleanest and best in the world (beware of the hot, which may come from natural thermal sources and smell faintly sulphurous). In the hills, clean spring water is usually safe to drink but avoid glacial meltwater.

PERSONAL SAFETY

Iceland is generally a safe country with a low crime rate, although petty crime is on the increase. Leave money and valuables in the hotel safe. Carry only what you need and keep it out of sight. On Friday and Saturday nights in central Reykjavík, and Akureyri, drunkenness can be a nuisance, but the mood is usually boisterous rather than violent.

TELEPHONES

Public telephones (sími) are usually found outside the post office. They take coins (10, 50 and 100kr) or phonecards – available from post offices/telephone stations.

International Dialling Codes

From Iceland to:

UK:	**00 44**
Germany:	**00 49**
USA & Canada:	**00 1**
Netherlands:	**00 31**

POST

Post offices are found in the main settlements around Iceland, opening hours are generally Mon–Fri 9–4:30. Stamps can also be bought in most souvenir outlets where postcards are sold. Icelandic stamps have a particular interest for collectors.

ELECTRICITY

The power supply in Iceland is: 220 volts, 50HZ. Sockets accept two-pin round plugs. UK visitors require a plug adaptor and US visitors will need a transformer for appliances operating on 100–120 volts.

● The Flybus link to Keflavík airport leaves from Hótel Loftleiðir approximately 2 hours before each flight, ☎ 562 1011. Cost ISK700. Free pick-up can be arranged from major hotels and guesthouses in the city. You can also check in luggage in advance – contact the number above for details. Don't forget to keep details handy for tax refunds on major purchases.

LANGUAGE

Icelandic is directly related to Old Norse and people with a knowledge of a Scandinavian language will therefore have a head start. For the rest of us, it's pretty impenetrable, but a limited guide to pronunciation will help the guesswork, especially when you are trying to find your way around the country. Two unfamiliar letters are: Ð/ð, pronounced as a hard th, as in then (Herðubreið), and Þ/þ (replaced by th in this book), pronounced as a soft, aspirated th, as in thistle (Thingvellir).

The letter j is pronounced as a y (for example, Jökulsárlón). When f is found before an l or n (for example, Hafnarfjörður) it is pronounced as p. The letter h takes on k-sound when in front of l, r or v (for example, Hlemmur).

When r is before l and n it takes on an extra d-sound (for example Perlan, which sounds like Perdlan).The double ll sounds rather like the Welsh equivalent, a soft 'kl' sound made somewhere in the back of the mouth (for example, Hellnar).

It's a relief to know that English is widely spoken, but even a few basic words of greeting will help to break down barriers.

hotel	hótel	guesthouse	gistihús
room	herbergi	toilet	klósett/salerni
single/double	fyrir einn/ fyrir tvo	view	útsýni
		campsite	tjaldsvæði
bank	banki	credit card	kreditkort
exchange office	exchange/banki	traveller's	ferðatékki
post office	póstur	cheque	
cash desk	afgreiðsla	passport	vegabréf
breakfast	morgunverður	beer	bjór
lunch	hádegismatur	coffee	kaffi
dinner	kvöldmatur	tea	te
restaurant	veitingahús	water	vatn
café	kaffihús	bread	brauð
menu	matseðill	fruit	ávöxtur
wine	vín	dessert	eftirréttur
aeroplane	flugvél	...port/harbour	höfn
airport	flugvöllur	ticket	miði
bus	strætisvagn	...single/return	aðra leið/ báðar leiðir
coach	rúta		
...station	stoppistöð/ strætisvagnastöð	car	bíll
		taxi	taxi
...stop	strætisvagnastopp	no smoking	ekki reykja
boat	bátur	timetable	tímatafla
yes/no	já/nei	where is...?	hvar er...?
please	gerðu það	my name is...	ég heiti...
thank you	takk	sorry	fyrirgefið
hello	hæ	excuse me	fyrirgefið
goodbye	bless/bæ	help!	hjálp!
good morning	góðan daginn	Sunday	sunnudagur
good evening	gótt kvöld	Monday	mánudagur
good night	góða nótt	Tuesday	þriðjudagur
I don't understand	ég skil ekki alveg	Wednesday	miðvikudagur
		Thursday	fimmtudagur
I don't speak Icelandic	ég tala ekki íslensku	Friday	föstudagur
		Saturday	laugardagur

INDEX

Acknowledgements
The Automobile Association would like to thank the following photographers and libraries for their assistance in the preparation of this book:

ARNI MAGNÚSSON INSTITUTE 36; ART DIRECTORS AND TRIP PHOTO LIBRARY 8b; BRUCE COLEMAN COLLECTION 49b, 65, 66t, 71t, 72t; EYE UBIQUITOUS 16b; THE ICELANDIC AD. AGENC 49c; THORARINN JONSSON 1, 7ct, 19b, 97; MATS WIBE LUND 5b, 43c; NATIONAL GALLERY OF ICELAND 33; PICTURES COLOUR LIBRARY 7b; REX FEATURES LTD 9b, 10b; SIGURGEIR SIGURJÓNSSON 15c, 17b, 40/41, 54/55, 62b, 63c, 63b, 69t; SPECTRUM COLOUR LIBRARY 30b; AN STONEHOUSE 2, 5t, 6t, 6b, 7t, 7cb, 8t, 9t, 10t, 10c, 11t, 12t, 12c, 13t, 13b, 14t, 15tr, 16t, 17t, 18t, 18b 19t, 20t, 20b, 21t, 22t, 22b, 23t, 23b, 24, 25, 26, 27, 28t, 28c, 29, 30t, 31r, 32, 33b, 34t, 34b, 37, 38t, 38 39t, 42t, 42b, 43c, 44t, 44c, 45t, 45b, 46t, 46r, 47t, 47c, 48t, 48c, 48b, 50, 51, 52, 53t, 53b, 54, 55, 56t, 5 57t, 57b, 58t, 58b, 59, 60t, 60b, 61t, 61b, 62t, 63t, 64, 66b, 67, 68, 69b, 70, 71b, 72b, 73t, 73b, 74, 75, 7 77, 78, 79, 80, 81, 82, 83, 84, 85, 86, 87b; WORLD PICTURES 11, 14/15, 15tl, 21b, 28/29, 31l, 35, 36/3 39b, 49t, 87t

Author's Acknowledgements
The author would like to thank the following people and companies for their help: Jóhann Thor Arnarsso Larus Thor Jóhannson; Avis; Michelle Boon at IcelandAir; Philip Brannigan; Dr Joachim Fischer; Vilborg Guðnadóttir at Tourist Information, Reykjavík; Jónas Helgason; Paul & Sigga Newton; Simon Sigurmonss & Svava Guðmundsdóttir; Sævar Skaptason at Icelandic Farm Holidays; Bernard & Sally Stonehouse; We Richards. And for the update: Jóhann Thor Arnarsson & Maria L Brynjolfsdottir; Sigurður D Thoroddsen; Sunna Arnadóttir & Gunnar St Gislason; Palmi Jonsson at Reykjavík Travel Service; Avis.

Copy editor: Gráinne Lenehan   Revision management: Pam Stagg

Dear Essential Traveller

Your comments, opinions and recommendations are very important to us. So please help us to improve our travel guides by taking a few minutes to complete this simple questionnaire.

You do not need a stamp (unless posted outside the UK). If you do not want to cut this page from your guide, then photocopy it or write your answers on a plain sheet of paper.

Send to: **The Editor, AA World Travel Guides, FREEPOST SCE 4598, Basingstoke RG21 4GY.**

Your recommendations…

We always encourage readers' recommendations for restaurants, nightlife or shopping – if your recommendation is used in the next edition of the guide, we will send you a *FREE* AA *Essential* **Guide** of your choice. Please state below the establishment name, location and your reasons for recommending it.

_____
_____
_____
_____

Please send me **AA *Essential*** _____
(see list of titles inside the front cover)

About this guide…

Which title did you buy?
AA *Essential* _____
Where did you buy it?_____
When? m m / y y

Why did you choose an AA *Essential* Guide? _____
_____
_____
_____
_____

Did this guide meet your expectations?
Exceeded ☐   Met all ☐   Met most ☐   Fell below ☐
Please give your reasons_____
_____
_____
_____

continued on next page…

Were there any aspects of this guide that you particularly liked? ___________

____

____

____

Is there anything we could have done better? ___________________

____

____

____

____

About you...

Name (*Mr/Mrs/Ms*) ______________________________

Address ______________________________

____

______________________ Postcode ______________

Daytime tel nos ______________________________

Which age group are you in?

Under 25 ☐ 25–34 ☐ 35–44 ☐ 45–54 ☐ 55–64 ☐ 65+ ☐

How many trips do you make a year?

Less than one ☐ One ☐ Two ☐ Three or more ☐

Are you an AA member? Yes ☐ No ☐

About your trip...

When did you book? m m / y y When did you travel? m m / y y

How long did you stay? ______________________________

Was it for business or leisure? ______________________________

Did you buy any other travel guides for your trip?

If yes, which ones? ______________________________

____

Thank you for taking the time to complete this questionnaire. Please send it to us as soon as possible, and remember, you do not need a stamp (*unless posted outside the UK*).

Happy Holidays!

The AA and the Automobile Association Limited, their subsidiaries and any other companies or bodies in which either has an interest ('the AA Group') may use information about you to provide you with details of other products and services, by telephone or in writing. The AA Group as a matter of policy does not release its lists to third parties.
If you do not wish to receive further information please tick the box... ☐

The Atlas

Thorarinn Jonsson: *if you plan to drive far into the interior a 4WD is essential*

The Automobile Association
www.theAA.com
The Automobile Association's website offers comprehensive and up-to-the-minute information covering AA-approved hotels, guest houses and B&Bs, restaurants and pubs in the UK; airport parking, insurance, European breakdown cover, European motoring advice, a ferry planner, European route planner, overseas fuel prices, a bookshop and much more.

The Foreign and Commonwealth Office
Country advice, traveller's tips, before you
go information, checklists and more.
www.fco.gov.uk

Iceland Tourist Board
www.icetourist.is

GENERAL
UK Passport Service
www.ukpa.gov.uk

Health Advice for Travellers
www.doh.gov.uk/traveladvice

UK Travel Insurance Directory
www.uktravelinsurancedirectory.co.uk

BBC – Holiday
www.bbc.co.uk/holiday

The Full Universal Currency Converter
www.xe.com/ucc/full.shtml

Flying with Kids
www.flyingwithkids.com

TRAVEL
Flights and Information
www.cheapflights.co.uk
www.thisistravel.co.uk
www.ba.com
www.icelandair.co.uk
www.worldairportguide.com

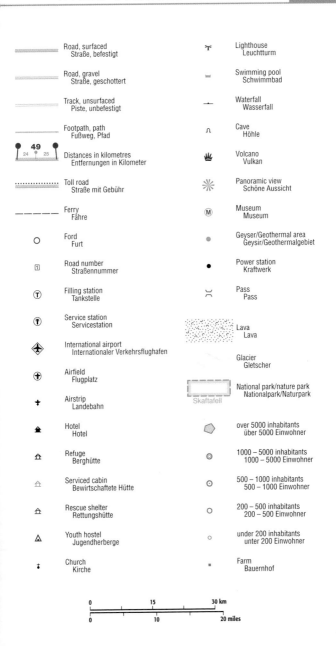

Road, surfaced	Straße, befestigt	Lighthouse	Leuchtturm
Road, gravel	Straße, geschottert	Swimming pool	Schwimmbad
Track, unsurfaced	Piste, unbefestigt	Waterfall	Wasserfall
Footpath, path	Fußweg, Pfad	Cave	Höhle
Distances in kilometres	Entfernungen in Kilometer	Volcano	Vulkan
Toll road	Straße mit Gebühr	Panoramic view	Schöne Aussicht
Ferry	Fähre	Museum	Museum
Ford	Furt	Geyser/Geothermal area	Geysir/Geothermalgebiet
Road number	Straßennummer	Power station	Kraftwerk
Filling station	Tankstelle	Pass	Pass
Service station	Servicestation	Lava	Lava
International airport	Internationaler Verkehrsflughafen	Glacier	Gletscher
Airfield	Flugplatz	National park/nature park	Nationalpark/Naturpark
Airstrip	Landebahn	Skaftafell	
Hotel	Hotel	over 5000 inhabitants	über 5000 Einwohner
Refuge	Berghütte	1000 – 5000 inhabitants	1000 – 5000 Einwohner
Serviced cabin	Bewirtschaftete Hütte	500 – 1000 inhabitants	500 – 1000 Einwohner
Rescue shelter	Rettungshütte	200 – 500 inhabitants	200 – 500 Einwohner
Youth hostel	Jugendherberge	under 200 inhabitants	unter 200 Einwohner
Church	Kirche	Farm	Bauernhof

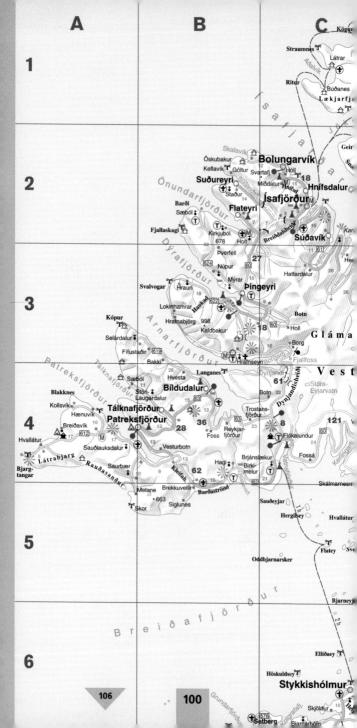

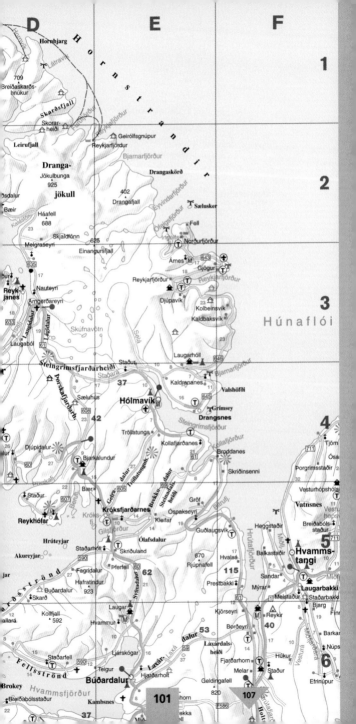

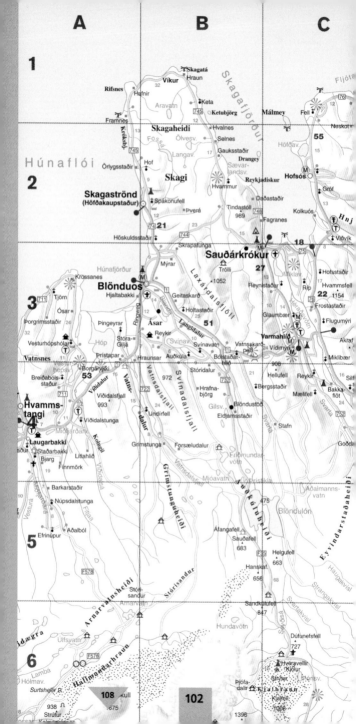

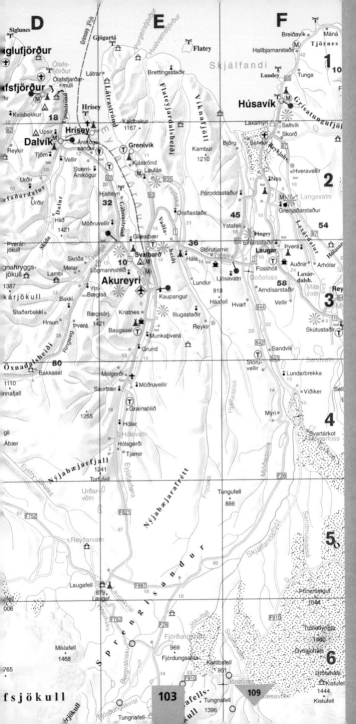

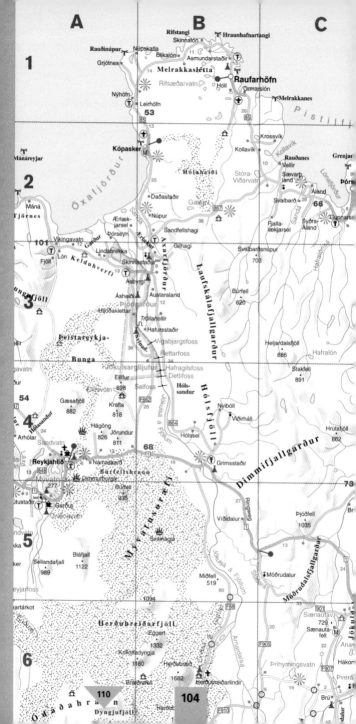

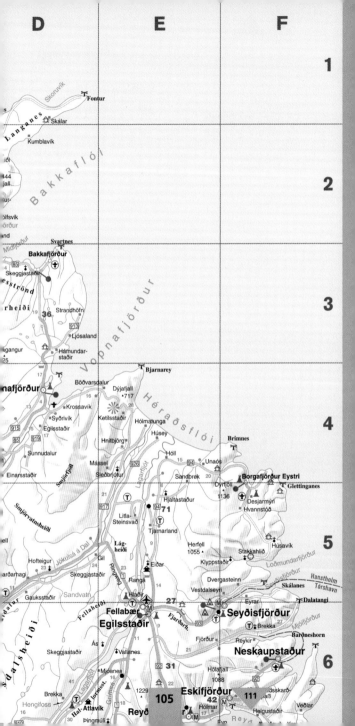

1

Dagverða
Elliðaey
Arney
Höskuldsey

Stykkishólmur

Skjöldur
Helgafell
Nar

Grundarfjörður

Setberg

Bjarnarhöfn

Klakkur

Berserkja-hraun

Búlands-höfði

Stóð 268

Kirgjuf.

67

Grundarfjörður

463

17

Ljósufjö

Hellisandur
Rif
Gufuskálar
Skarðs

Ólafsvík

Ingjaldshóll

Fróðá

S n æ f e l l s n e s

Hjaðarfell
Miðhraun
Fáskrúðarb

Neshraun
Helja

Fróðáheiði

778
Helgrundur
Mælifell
566

58

Ellíðatindar
Vegamót

Þjóðgarður
Snæfellsjökull

1446

Gröf
Knörr

Lýsuhóll
Garðar

Mikilholt

25

Hólahólar
Snæfells-jökull
579

Stapafr

Búðir
Búðah.

Staðarstaður

13

2

Dritvík

Hellnar

Arnarstapi

Stakkhamar

Skógarnes

Malarrif
Löndrangar

Haffjörð

Hvalseyjar

3

F a x a f l ó

4

A T L A N T S -

H A F

Garðskagi

Garður

Sandgerði

Keflaví

Hvalsnes

Njarðvík

Stafnes

Hafn

Hafnaberg

12

Reykjanes

5

Reykjanestá

G

Eldey

6

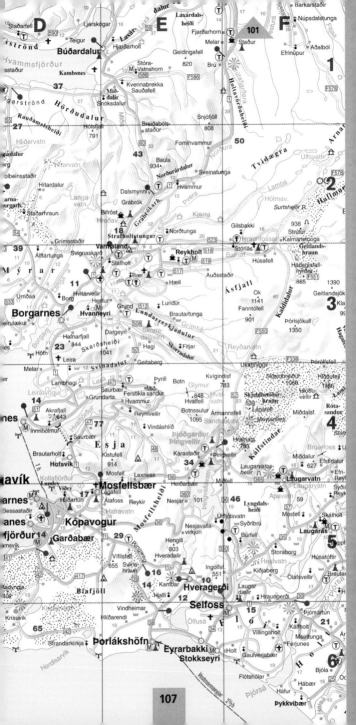

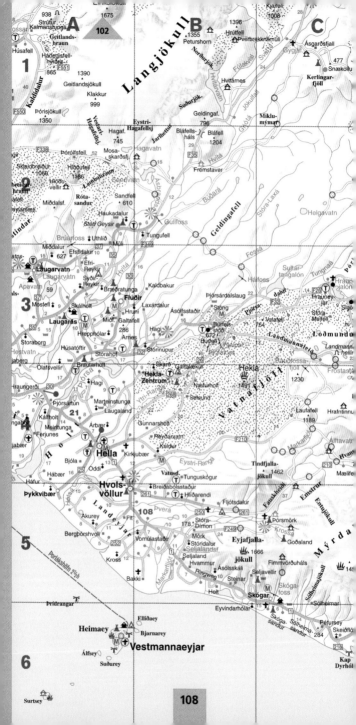

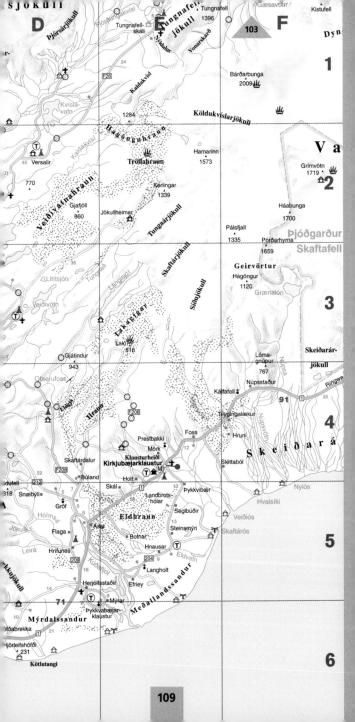

SJÖKULL

Þjórsárjökull

Tungnafell 1396

Gæsavötn

Kistufell

Dyn

D

Þjórsárjökull

Tungnafell-skáli

Tungnafell-jökull

Nýidalur

Vonarskarð

103

F

1

24

F26

Kaldakvísl

Bárðarbunga
2009

Kvísla-vatn

1284

Köldukvíslarjökull

Versalir
45

Kaldakvísl

Hágönguhraun

Tröllahraun

Hamarinn
1573

V a

Grímvötn
1719

2

770

Gjáfjöll
860

Veiðivatnahraun

Kerlingar
1339

Jökullheimar

Háabunga
1700

Litlisjón
35

Tungnaá

Langisjór

Tungnaárjökull

Skaftárjökull

Síðujökull

Pálsfjall
1335

Þórðarhyma
1659

Þjóðgarður
Skaftafell

Geirvörtur

Hágöngur
1120

Grænalón

3

Veiðivötn

Lakagígar

Gjátindur
943

Laki
818

Lómagnúpur
767

Skeiðarár-jökull

Öræfufoss

Eldgjá

Hnappur

F206

Núpsstaður

Kálfafell

Núpsvötn

Ringwe

91

1

35

Skaftárdalur

Búland

F208

Prestbakki

Mörk

Klausturheiði
Kirkjubæjarklaustur

Foss

Hruni

Teygingalækur

Sléttaból

Skeiðará

4

Snæbýli
318

212

22

Gröf

5

7

Hólmar

Flaga

Ása

Skál

Holt

1

Landbrots-hólar

Pykkvibær

Seglbúðir

Steinsmýri

13

Nyilós

Hvalsíki

Veiðiós

Skaftárós

Eldhraun

Botnar

Hnausar

204

Langholt

Efriey

5

Leirá

Hrífunes

208

Kúðafljót

16

Herjólfsstaðir

Eldvatn

Meðallandssandur

71

Mýrar

Pykkvabæjar-klaustur

Myrdalssandur

ðabrekka
10

1

21

Hjörleifshöfði
231

Kötlutangi

6

A
104
B
C
1
2
3
4
5
6
Kollóttadyngja
1180
Herðubreið
1682
Bræðrafell
Herðubreiðarlindir
Þríhyrningsvatn
F907
Brú
Ódáðahraun
Dyngjufjöll
Herðubreiðartögl
1073
F910
Goðahraun
Víti
Öskjuv.
Askja
Dreki
Víkursandur
Upptyppingar
925
Kreppa
Reykjará
Meljaðrafjall
Hrafnkelsdalur
1510
1172
Þorvaldstindur
Dyngjuv.
Vaðalda
941
Krepputunga
Jökulsá á Fjöllum
Jökulsá á Brú
F902
F903
Grágæsavatn
Vestur-dalsvötn
Holuhraun
Urðarháls
Kistufell
1444
F909
Snæfell
1833
Vesturöræfi
Snæfellsskáli
Karlfell
1132
Virkisf.
1108
Biskupsfell
Maríutungur
Dyngjujökull
Sigurðarskáli
Kverkfjöll
1860
Kverkjökull
1929
Brúarjökull
Eyjabakkajökull
Goðahnúkar
Hoffellsjökull
Vatnajökull
Norðlingalægð
Fláajökull
Heinabergsjökull
Skálafellsjökull
Esjufjöll
1522
F985
Borgarhöfn
Ringweg
Snæfell
1383
Kálfafellsstaður
Þjóðgarður
Skaftafell
Þverártindur
1113
Steinasandur
Mávabiggdir
Steinafjall
Reynivellir
Breiðamerkurjökull
Jökulsárlón
Svartifoss
1126
Skaftafell
Skaftafellsjökull
Öræfajökull
774
Hrollaugseyjar
2119
Hvannadalshnúkur
Svínafell
Kvísker
Breiðamerkursandur
Hof
Hnappavellir
Öræfi
Fagurhólsmýri
Skeiðará
Skeiðarársandur
Leirur
Ingólfshöfði

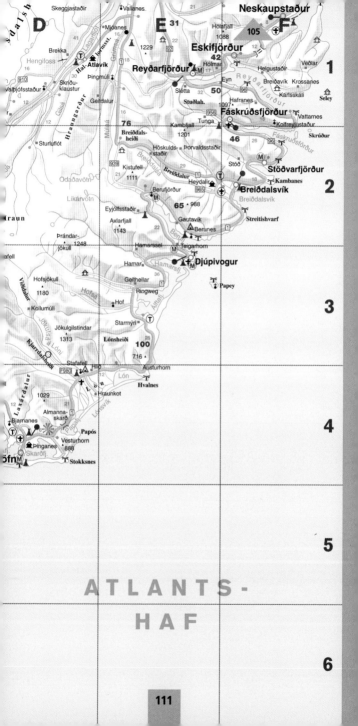

ATLANTS-
HAF

111